CLIMBERS
AND CLEMATIS

CLIMBERS
AND CLEMATIS

Plants for Window Boxes, Hanging Baskets,
Containers, Pots and Tubs

CAROLINE BOISSET

BOOKMART LIMITED

CLIMBERS AND CLEMATIS
Caroline Boisset

To my parents, Claude and Bernard Boisset

First published in 1988 by Mitchell Beazley,
an imprint of Reed Consumer Books Limited
Michelin House, 81 Fulham Road, London SW3 6RB
and Auckland, Melbourne, Singapore and Toronto

This edition published in 1994 by Reed Consumer Books
for Bookmart Limited

A catalogue record for this book is available at the British Library

ISBN 0-86363-046-4

The publishers have made every effort to ensure that all instructions given
in this book are accurate and safe, but they cannot accept liability for any
resulting injury, damage or loss to either person or property whether direct
or consequential and howsoever arising. The author and publishers will be
grateful for any information which will assist them in keeping future editions
up to date.

Printed by Graficas Estella, Spain

CONTENTS

"Vertical gardening offers more than a solution to the problem of limited space. It also provides excellent possibilities to those who have a passionate interest in individual plants of all types and love the challenge of coaxing the best from them by patient observation and care."

INTRODUCTION

In any style of garden, there are many advantages in extending upwards. A living screen of flowers or foliage, perhaps a trellis woven with clematis or climbing roses or honeysuckle, encourages maximum beauty from minimum space. It offers an excellent way to block out, wholly or partially, an unwanted view, to add interest to the blank, boring wall of the house, or to divide the garden into compartments, each with its own distinct mood.

Making a screen is just one of a whole repertoire of ways to garden vertically. At a fairly simple level, you can decorate a wall with window boxes and hanging baskets to present a superb display that changes through the seasons. Or, more ambitiously, you can change the contours of your garden: a terrace with a retaining wall presents a greater surface for gardening, and a wider range of growing conditions, than are offered by a continuous slope. Even water can be introduced into the vertical garden – although, of course, you will need a pump to recycle it between levels.

Traditionally, gardens are thought of in plan. Many of the great gardens of the past, with their elaborate arrangements of parterres, turned the ground surface into massive geometrical patterns. These days, few gardeners have anything like the space for this lavishness. In a small garden, making full use of perpendicular surfaces enables us to compose a picture, or series of pictures, that entirely fills our view and creates a sense of seclusion – all on a relatively small scale. Not least of the advantages of this style of gardening is that you can make the plot seem larger than it is – the technique of suggestion by concealment, which is one of the aspects I consider in the pages that follow. Another, more blatant type of illusion is the use of mirrors or *trompe l'œil* trelliswork or even wall paintings to increase the sense of depth.

Walls, hedges and fences not only provide privacy and visual interest in themselves, they also enable you to vary the climatic conditions, so that you can grow a wide range of plants in the same plot. Vertical gardening thus offers more than a solution to the problem of limited space. It also provides excellent possibilities to those who, like myself, have a passionate interest in individual plants of all types and love the challenge of coaxing the best from them by patient observation and care.

FIRST PRINCIPLES

Vertical gardening, like any other kind of gardening, demands a knowledge of the habit, flowering characteristics and growing requirements of a wide range of plants. First, you need to decide on the style or mood that you want to achieve, and devise an overall plan that provides the necessary level of variety and seclusion. Only then should you choose the individual plants, taking into account the soil of your plot, the pattern of light and shade, the time you are willing to spend on maintenance, and the need for a changing display that will provide interest at all times of year.

VERTICAL STYLES

Country-dwellers usually aim for a garden that blends with and borrows from the surrounding landscape. Many city folk frown with envy, likening their tiny backyard or patio to a miniature desert. In fact, they have the challenge of a more or less blank canvas to work on. In a garden where vertical surfaces dominate, you can control almost every aspect of the view.

The most successful gardens are those with a distinct mood or style, and with the sense of inevitability that comes from decisive planning. It helps to work your way through an imaginary questionnaire. Do you want the garden to be formal or informal? Will the emphasis be on the plants or on the hard surfaces? Will ornament play a significant role? Will the planting be soft and romantic or do you prefer a crisp, graphic look? Of course, all these questions are tied in with more practical concerns – notably, the maintenance factor.

The "cottage garden" style has vivid appeal. The words conjure an image of roses, honey-

suckle and clematis tumbling over the porch, old walls with nooks and crannies colonized by all sorts of alpines – and perhaps bright annuals and lovely spring bulbs in terracotta pots, hanging baskets and cast-off chimney pots. The prominence of climbers in this archetypal garden allows it to be recreated even within the dimensions of a handkerchief plot. Scent is also a main ingredient, easily introduced with a fragrant old rose near a window. To sustain the traditional mood, choose old-fashioned, pre-hybrid plants in preference to modern varieties.

Instead of cottage-garden profusion, you might prefer a more formal effect against a background of clipped and disciplined hedges. Small-leaved species of hedging plant are most suitable for this treatment. Combined with urns and statuary, they can evoke the grand historic gardens of France and Italy. Renaissance and Baroque styles of ornament are available today in simulated stone: some are accurate reproductions of authentic carved deities, pineapples, and baskets of fruit; others are travesties. A single

Vertical gardens often depend on a contrast of foliage and flowers against the colour and texture of walls.

LEFT *In this Italianate courtyard, plants clustered together in an enclosed, sheltered space around a fountain and a graceful statue create a sense of almost tropical lushness. Blue-flowering plumbago, ivy, yellow abutilon and jasmine climb the walls; pelargoniums grow in delicate baskets which echo the bowls of the fountain; and on the ground in pots are Hedychium, camellias and Sparmannia.*

FAR LEFT *The exuberance of the courtyard garden (left) will not be to everyone's taste. Provided that the architecture is of high quality, a simpler, sparser effect can be just as pleasing. On the opposite page a climbing rose of considerable character and strong colouring graces a semi-circular alcove. The impact depends on the wayward, meandering form of the rose, contrasting with the strict geometry of the stonework.*

high-quality sculptural feature such as a carved waterspout on a boundary wall can be used as the focus of a stunning formal composition. In a small plot you can afford to use the very best plants and materials.

Historic and exotic garden styles may suggest a starting point for design, but there is no need to swallow such influences whole. For example, tight bamboo fencing backing a rectangle of raked gravel will carry strong connotations of Japan. Bolstering the theme further by the inclusion of a stone lantern against the bamboo might be regarded as labouring the point. On the other hand, a Renaissance-style urn in the same position would strike a decidedly wrong note. It is arguably better not to communicate at all than to send out conflicting signals.

A thematic approach can also be adopted in the planting. All-white gardens are deservedly popular, and can work well regardless of the permanent materials that form the plot's framework – although white against a dark green yew hedge is a little too startling for comfort. Two-colour schemes, against a background of green, might be chosen as a more varied palette. Contrasts of foliage texture also make a good basis for a design. Alternatively, your criterion for selecting plants might be geographical – perhaps with the emphasis on climbers and shrubs from China, such as *Abelia chinensis*, *Clematis armandii* and *Wisteria sinensis*.

Whatever style you choose, its precise embodiment will be influenced by certain constraints, including climate, soil, money and the time you can spend on upkeep. Another factor is the use to which the garden will be put – seating requirements, creation of shady or sunny areas, and so on. Although these factors may be restrictive, they will help you by reducing what might otherwise be a bewildering range of planting options. Within those limits, you will have ample freedom to express yourself.

A single dramatic plant can often be more effective than a mass of less striking ones. In each of these three examples the choice of plant is exactly right for the situation.

FAR LEFT *A single columnar cactus is clearly defined against the unadorned, white-painted wall of a modernistic house in California.*

CENTRE *The red form of the virgin's bower – Clematis viticella 'Rubra' – is a happy match for the weathered brick of a gate pier, creating a mood of cottage garden charm. The clematis will flower profusely throughout the summer and can be left to scramble freely across the wall as it requires only a minimum of pruning.*

LEFT *Flowering shrubs grown as standards are well-suited to pot culture, and can look dramatic against a house wall. This plant is the crape myrtle (*Lagerstroemia indica*), its blooms making a cheerful contrast with blue shutters. If not trained, it would grow to 24 feet (8m) or more. It does best in mild climates, but when pot-grown can easily be brought indoors for the winter if necessary.*

THE QUESTION OF MAINTENANCE

RIGHT *This small medium-maintenance garden would be ideal for someone who enjoys easy routine tasks but lacks the time or inclination for prolonged labour. The wall and its superstructure of white-painted slats is being slowly covered with virginia creeper, which from time to time will need to be cut back selectively to ensure that it does not swamp its background and detract from the shelf-mounted, shrub-filled window boxes. The shrubs are mainly evergreen, and include the golden variegated Elaeagnus pungens 'Maculata', a camellia which will flower in early spring and a low-growing juniper. Planted close together for a full, mature effect, these shrubs will need careful control in a few years time, or they will begin to crowd each other out.*

No garden, however well designed, will look good unless regularly and correctly maintained. This applies as much to a patio flanked by trellis-grown climbers and hanging baskets as it does to a spacious garden of lawns and borders. Many people mistakenly believe that plants will look after themselves. In reality, they quickly deteriorate; after a year or two some look messy, some a sickly yellow, while others slow down in their growth and eventually die or succumb to an attack of fungus.

True gardeners will find that simple routine tasks of maintenance offer their own satisfactions. Weeding, deadheading, hedge trimming and pruning are not demanding, particularly in a small garden, and are therefore therapeutic. Time spent in the garden is also time in which to watch plants develop and assess their requirements so that you can take action punctually, whether they need pruning, or feeding, or delivering from an onslaught of greenfly.

The design of a garden is only as good as its maintenance regime. So, before you launch into a grand and intricate design, give some thought to the amount of time you are willing to spend on looking after it. Make out a list of all the tasks that need to be done and plan how and when you will be able to do them.

If you decide that, initially at least, you are able to perform only minimum labour, keep the design simple. Choose plants that are reasonably slow-growing and use sculpture, or pots filled with bulbs, annuals or perennials that can easily be changed or need repotting infrequently, as the chief components of your design. Bear in mind, however, that the initial capital input of a low-maintenance garden is inevitably fairly high.

The patio garden is the epitome of this style of gardening. Paved surfaces only need an occasional sweep to remove debris. Raised beds can be planted with climbers and wall shrubs mixed with low growing perennials and spring bulbs; annuals grown in pots that can be moved with ease can provide additional colour at different seasons. Deadheading and watering will be the only maintenance tasks necessary, provided that all the plants have been initially potted in good compost.

For the walls, choose self-clinging climbers that will not require tying in and plant some low-growing sub-shrubs that only need pruning once a year at the beginning of the growing season; for example, *Hydrangea petiolaris* edged with santolina. For variety, another area of the garden could be planted with low herbaceous perennials interplanted with spring-flowering bulbs – for example, *Alchemilla mollis* mixed with daffodils and tulips.

Most bulbs make excellent low-maintenance plants because all they need is deadheading after they have flowered and an annual top dressing of a well-balanced slow-release fertilizer. The santolina would need cutting back hard in late spring and the hydrangea may need trimming occasionally once it has become well established. However, in this planting plan the only additional task would be watering. This is essential while the plants are establishing themselves and thereafter whenever the soil becomes very dry – alchemilla obligingly droops when it needs water and cheers up very quickly once the dose has been administered.

Using the right tools is all-important for ease of maintenance. In the vertical garden probably one of the most important tools is the ladder or steps. Many climbers grow to over 7 or 8 feet (2– 2.25m), over roofs and round corners that will be out of comfortable reach. Consequently you should choose a ladder that has a wide base and will be safe to work from, particularly if you do not have someone else around who can steady the base while you are working. Remember always to choose a level spot to stand it on.

LEFT *By placing the emphasis on sculptural and architectural details, you can reduce the maintenance requirements of a garden without compromising the overall impact. If you use a strong piece of sculpture as the focal point, it would be a mistake to surround it with too much competing detail. Here, an elegant wall fountain is framed simply by trailing stems of* Lespedeza thunbergii. *This member of the pea family does best in warm, dry situations and enjoys the well-drained, sunny environment to be found at the top of a wall. In cold climates it is cut back to the woody rootstock every winter but grows back again in the spring. Small pods, borne in the autumn, each contain one viable seed which can be used for propagation; alternatively, the plant can be divided in spring.*

"Labour-saving" tools, if properly used, will enable you to be slightly more adventurous in your design without adding significantly to the time spent in maintenance. Electric hedge trimmers are useful if you have long lengths of hedges. Long-handled clippers work well, especially on soft material, and spring-loaded gadgets are now available for lowering and raising hanging baskets, which makes watering or deadheading so much easier.

RIGHT *A climbing rose will happily push beyond the roof line if you let it. There is little harm in this, except that you will need a ladder for pruning and you may often have to clear the gutter of leaves. More vigorous, self-clinging climbers cannot be allowed such freedom, as they have a tendency to grow under eaves and roof tiles, causing potential damage to the structure. Always check the growth rate before planting a self-clinger alongside the house.*

In my experience, gardening is a pastime that often turns into a passion as you get to know your plants better. As you find yourself willing to devote more time to work in the garden, the design and plant content can become more ambitious and diverse. You will know that you have reached this stage when you actually look forward to spending an hour or two in the evenings weeding, tying in and pruning climbers, watering pots and growing new plants.

As you make this transition you will eventually come up against what is, probably, the most demanding task in the vertical garden: pruning. Even here there are degrees of difficulty.

Roses, generally, need very little pruning except to remove old branches and any that threaten to grow out of reach or obstruct windows; but they will need regular tying in. Clematis, on the other hand, are self-supporting but vary in their pruning requirements. Broadly speaking, clematis divide into three groups: those that flower on the previous year's wood need light pruning and shaping immediately after flowering; those that flower on short stems growing from the previous season's leaf axil buds need pruning back, in the early spring, to a strong pair of buds on all stems; and those that flower on the current season's growth need cutting right back, in the early spring, to just above the previous season's growth, about $2\frac{1}{2}$ feet (50cm) off the ground.

Complicated as this may sound, you will be surprised how quickly you learn the basic principles. This process of learning something new each season or each year is the essence of gardening. Few pleasures compare to that of assisting in the continual development of different plants throughout the growing season and into winter, and then looking forward to the following spring, knowing that no two years in the garden are ever the same.

LEFT AND ABOVE *When climbers are combined with container plants, as in both gardens here, the maintenance requirements can be considerable. The large-flowered clematis (both pictures) and the grapevine (left) need annual pruning and retraining to maintain a pleasing balance. The pot-grown annuals and herbaceous perennials (including heliotropes and pelargoniums on the stairs, right) will need watering daily through the summer, as the soil dries out faster in pots than in the ground. Despite this claim on time, pots are invaluable, allowing plants to be over-wintered indoors in areas susceptible to frost.*

SUN AND SHELTER

Building walls and growing hedges around a garden will protect it from wind or sun and from rain and alter its microclimate considerably, both at ground level and higher up.

Traditionally, walled gardens were built with the two longest walls facing north and south. In this configuration the temperature could differ by as much as 10°C (18°F) between these two wall faces. On the warmer side, the growing season would be extended at both ends to ensure that fruit was available for longer periods. The heat from the sun's rays, absorbed by the bricks during the day and radiated out during the night, increases the mean temperature and reduces the fluctuation between day and night-time temperatures. This was an important technique in the days when storage was not as sophisticated as it is today.

It was also well understood that if a cold wind got into the garden it could be trapped, resulting in a significant temperature reduction and damage to the plants from dehydration. To give protection from this effect, windbreaks of poplar, larch, spruce or pine were planted in a strategic position to filter and dissipate the prevailing winds before they hit the outside of the wall and eddied into the garden.

This problem rarely occurs in towns where the temperature is generally higher and where surrounding buildings break the wind's velocity. However, very tall buildings create local turbulence, against which there is no easy remedy. In a country garden, hedges and groups of trees will filter the wind and prevent any build up of cold air. If you have a wall that is exposed to the wind you should ensure that the more delicate climbers and wall shrubs are planted in the most protected position, right against the wall, and secured tightly. Alternatively, you could choose very hardy, strong-growing climbers that are self-clinging.

ABOVE *Many of the shade-tolerant plants suitable for dark corners have vivid green leaves that will brighten an otherwise dull space. Here, the primitive small leaves of the helxine have been allowed to form a dense mat against which the golden leaves of* Lamium maculatum 'Aureum' *seem all the brighter. The feathery fronds of the fern provide additional interest.*

Walls and hedges also have the effect of blocking out light. The shade is greatest at the bottom of the wall and on those walls that face north and east in the northern hemisphere, and south and east in the southern. These areas are ideally suited to the planting of woodland climbers, such as honeysuckles, *Celastrus orbiculatus*, *Pileostegia viburnoides* and *Berberidopsis corallina* – plants that in their natural habitat are shaded from direct sunlight by taller trees. If you want to grow plants that need more sunny conditions you can heighten the walls using a trellis that allows light in from both sides. It also follows that the soil at the base of shady walls is less likely to dry out as fast as that at the base of sunny walls, so choose plants that grow naturally in cool, moist soils.

Warm sunny walls should be used to best advantage. Don't waste them by growing the more ordinary wall shrubs and climbers. Instead, seek out the unusual. You could try, for example, the bright, orange-flowered, trumpet vine *Campsis radicans*; *Solanum crispum* 'Glasnevin', a beautiful climber related to the potato; *Piptanthus laburnifolius*, an evergreen shrub of the legume family, with bright yellow, pea-shaped flowers set against deep green leaves; or *Clematis cirrhosa balearica*, a winter-flowering plant with fern-like leaves which are green in summer and a striking bronze-purple in autumn. All four can be grown in colder climates provided that they are planted in the warmest spot in the garden – usually a sunny, sheltered corner. You should prune them all in the spring, in the process removing frost-damaged shoots; autumn pruning would leave new shoots at the mercy of winter cold. At the base of the wall, plant bulbs that enjoy a summer baking (such as *Nerines* and *Crinum*) or some of the South African herbaceous perennials that, in winter, need a dry, well-drained soil (for example, *Diascia rigescens* or *Osteospermum ecklonis*).

LEFT *Shady narrow backyards can be used as secluded retreats, but you must choose the plants with care, taking into account the varying pattern of light and shade throughout the day. In this garden (shown here at the only time of day when sun penetrates), potted ivies stand near the house, with ferns in the dark, damp corners.*

Blooms of early-flowering species may be spoilt after a cold night if they are grown on a wall that is warmed too fiercely by the early morning sun. Thus, you should choose a reasonably well-lit but shady wall for clematis cultivars 'Barbara Jackman', 'John Warren', 'Nelly Moser' and 'Lincoln Star' or roses 'Madame Alfred Carrière', 'Veilchenblau' and 'Parkdirektor Riggers'. Among winter-flowering species that give their best on shady walls are *Jasminum nudiflorum*, *Forsythia suspensa* and the ever-greens *Garrya elliptica* and *Euonymus fortunei*.

It is always difficult to cope with walls that are in the shade of other walls or buildings. They receive nearly no light and very little water, the atmosphere surrounding them is often still and dank and the soil beneath either insalubrious or non-existent. About the only plants that will survive these rigorous conditions are the more vigorous members of the ivy (*Hedera*) family. Choose variegated ones that will brighten the space, such as *Hedera helix* 'Adam', which has pinky variegation in winter, 'Glacier', which has white variegation, and 'Goldheart', which has a yellow centre to the leaf. *Hedera colchica* 'Dentata Variegata' is a bigger-leaved ivy that is equally suitable. It is also worth trying *Parthenocissus quinquefolia*, the virginia creeper, which has a glorious display of colour as the summer wanes; and *P. tricuspidata*, the Boston ivy, which tolerates even the most unpromising city conditions.

In these dark situations, the secret is to ensure that the plant is given a good start as it will grow strongly once established. Choose a nice healthy-looking plant when you buy it and be sure to dig in a good quantity of new compost when you put it in the ground. Choose the spot that receives the most light, even if it is a little further away from where you want the plant to grow. When it is growing strongly you will gradually be able to guide it across the wall.

LEFT *In this warm sunny corner, palms and bougainvilleas give a subtropical feel. These are tender plants which need protection from frost. In hot climates where there is sufficient irrigation, bougainvillea grows very fast and, if it is to be contained, needs frequent pruning – a task that must be performed with care, as the plant climbs by hooked thorns which also act as a defence against grazing animals.*

ABOVE *The bright purple mass of bougainvillea in this garden is unmistakable. The vivid colour, however, is not in the flowers (which are white and inconspicuous) but in the modified leaves, or bracts. Above, on the terrace, are three forms of the Mediterranean oleander (*Nerium oleander*): one pink, one red and one white. In temperate or continental climates, these are all suitable for growing in pots that can be brought in from the cold during the winter.*

A few clematis cultivars (such as rosy-mauve Clematis chrysocoma *and white or cream C. florida 'Sieboldii') need to be grown on a warm, sunny wall, but many are best suited to a cool, shady position.*

RIGHT *A white large-flowered clematis frames a doorway. The blooms are growing toward the light, but the roots are in the shade – a requisite for all clematis cultivars.*

FAR RIGHT *This purple large-flowered clematis is shown receiving its afternoon dose of sunshine: for most of the day it is in shade. Many blue and purple clematis cultivars risk having their flowers bleached if they receive direct sun. One of the exceptions to this broad rule is 'Ernest Markham', which needs a sunny wall.*

COLOUR AND THE SEASONS

Colour can be a perplexing issue for the vertical gardener – the yardstick where taste is measured and can so easily fail to please. The problem – which, of course, is more constructively seen as an exciting challenge – is the sheer range of hues available. Some permutations look indisputably wrong, others triumphantly right. Steering a course through the huge range of options may at first result in bewilderment, but this will change as in time you develop experience and a more confident eye.

Even a single category of plants can encompass an enormous colour range. Clematis offers blues, purples, reds, yellows and white; while the colours of climbing roses are a subject for study in themselves, ranging from subtle shades of old roses (like the mélange of peach, buff and apricot in 'Gloire de Dijon') to the more vivid effects of modern strains. Within a narrow band of the spectrum, different shades may present a complete contrast of mood. A gardener who favours the deep crimson-scarlet of the 'Ena Harkness' rose may find the carmine of 'Parade' excessively redolent of the boudoir. Even greens present a wealth of different shades, some of them surprisingly vibrant.

Faced with such a varied palette, you must choose with care. The appearance of colours is always affected by the surrounding colours – an important factor, because it enables you to manipulate colour schemes to achieve a particular effect. Often, a successful picture can be created more readily by a restrained approach than by boldness and brio. Vivid polychrome displays have their place (especially in window boxes, to cheer up a dull frontage), but are not recommended if the aim is to create a secluded, restful enclave. The function of most gardens is to soothe rather than to stimulate.

There are often good and objective reasons why particular colour mixes work or don't work.

To understand more about these reasons, it helps to know a little about the science of colour.

Red and blue flowers together will fight in a scheme and never create a happy picture. In scientific terms, this is because they have wavelengths at opposite ends of the spectrum and the eye has difficulty in adjusting to the combination. However, if you reduce the intensities of these colours to pink and pale blue, they will associate successfully. Because of their short wavelength, blues seem to recede into the distance; on the other hand, red, with its long wavelength, will seem to advance against a background of foliage. This phenomenon can be used to advantage in the vertical garden. For example, a screen of blue flowers or bluish or greyish foliage will appear farther away than it is – an effect that you can use to make a small patio or terrace appear less confined. Red flowers or berries, conversely, will provide vivid accents of colour that seem to clamour for notice. Yellows and oranges also seem to press themselves on the viewer's attention.

The quality of light has an important effect on the way in which we perceive colours. In bright sunshine, pale-coloured flowers may dwindle into insignificance. On the other hand, soft, watery light will make bright, vivid colours look

An area of the vertical garden could be devoted to a single flower colour. For example, the blue and mauve plants on these pages will flower in succession from spring to summer.

FAR LEFT *The large-flowered clematis hybrid 'Lasurstern' flowers in early summer for several weeks.*

CENTRE *The Inshriach form of* Clematis alpina *has nodding, bell-shaped flowers.*

ABOVE Wisteria sinensis *is often slow to flower at first. Encourage by cutting back the long shoots in mid-summer, after flowering, and in winter pruning the side shoots to four or five buds from the base. Try pairing with yellow* Rosa banksiae.

vulgarly gaudy. Hence, climate must be taken into account. The high sunlight of tropical or sub-tropical regions calls for assertive hues, whereas in cooler latitudes, where the light is more subtle, pastels come into their own. Similarly, the amount of shade in the garden is part of the equation. Against a shady wall, white flowers will glow luminously, whereas reds will lose some of their strength, appearing almost black as the shadows deepen toward the end of the day.

When planning colour for the garden, remember to take account of permanent features such as walls, seats and ornaments. The architectural framework of the plot is usually an unalterable given – a baseline for design. This is especially true of brick and stone walls. Brickwork varies enormously in colour, and plants to be grown against brick should be chosen with care. For example, pink- and white-flowered roses go well on a mellow red brick surface, but where the brick is more orange it is better to choose yellow, buff or orangey cultivars. Grey stone makes a good foil for vividly coloured blooms.

There are some garden structures that can be either treated with reticence, to the point of invisibility, or used to make a bold colour statement, depending on personal taste and the planting with which they are juxtaposed. A notable instance of this is trelliswork. In natural browns, trellises disappear among the foliage to which they act as a host. However, by painting a trellis you can make a graphic diamond pattern to offset the colour and natural form of the planting.

Colour, of course, is never perceived in isolation. When we look at colours we are always looking at textures simultaneously, and what the eye sees is an integrated effect. Texture even

FAR LEFT *The virginia
creeper is well-loved for
its vivid autumn tints.
Here, against an old
wooden fence, it
weaves through the
silvery seed heads of
Clematis tangutica.
Green leaves of wild
bindweed make a
striking contrast.*

*The colours of dying
leaves, berries and seed
heads all contribute to
autumn's atmosphere.
Climbers and wall
shrubs offer unlimited
possibilities.*

CENTRE *Pyracantha,
the firethorn (shown
here with a variegated
ivy), is hardy and
tolerant of pollution. It
is often grown in cities,
where its berries
brighten many a drab
wall. As well as red-
berried P. atalantioides
and P. 'Watereri'
there are orange and
yellow-berried varieties.*

BELOW *The rough, bold
textures of large-leaved
Vitis coignetiae show
autumn colours against
the bark of an old elm.
The foliage passes
through golden to
crimson, eventually
making a dramatic
wall of flame.*

ABOVE *Summer is never far away when the angular grey branches of* Chaenomeles × superba *'Knap Hill Scarlet' begin to burst into colour. Here, the deep red flowers harmonize with weathered bricks.*

FAR RIGHT *A strong red form of the houseleek,* Semper-vivum tectorum, *growing with a host of offsets, resembles a group of sea anemones. The stone wall provides the ideal well-drained, sunny environment.*

RIGHT *The fascinating concentric blooms of the passion flower (*Passiflora caerulea), *together with its blue-tinged, deeply-lobed leaves, always bring a touch of the exotic to the garden. If planted in a sheltered spot, this plant is particularly vigorous, attaching itself by twining tendrils. The egg-shaped, yellow fruit will ripen only after a long hot summer.*

affects the way we discern colour: for example, smooth or waxy leaves appear darker, while furry ones appear lighter. When planning plant combinations you always need to consider colour and texture in tandem.

The use of wall shrubs and climbers of differing texture will create ever-changing patterns, and form an interesting background for flowering plants. Large, boldly textured and patterned leaves such as the pink, white and green foliage of *Actinidia kolomikta* will create a focus on a wall amid other, smaller-leaved climbers such as roses, honeysuckles and clematis or *Myrtus communis* and *Abeliophyllum distichum*. Hedges, too, can be enhanced by interplanting the dominant species with a compatible climber. For example, the beautiful

flame nasturtium, *Tropaeolum speciosum*, associates well with yew or holly. The pale green, lobed leaves of the nasturtium will creep up the shady side of the hedge, counterpointing its deep green leaves and tempering its crisp hard texture to a much softer effect.

It is well known that container plants offer opportunities for bright colour accents in summer, though for a small plot I would counsel against being over-ambitious. One year I grew an assortment of annuals for the patio and, in my enthusiasm, ended up with rather a lot of different colours to accommodate in a tiny space. I lived with the result for that one summer but it wasn't the sort of scheme I would like to have every year and I have since learned to discipline myself: the smaller the garden, the more

selective one has to be in the planting.

I now find that simple solutions are always the best for small areas. Use bold foliage, planted in strong lines, to articulate the intended structure of the garden, hiding any undesirable features. This backdrop can be punctuated and underlined by a few harmonizing containers and pots. Choose those that are made either from similar materials to your walls or in toning colours – greys, stone, bluey greens or palest pinks are among the best, depending on the surroundings and the plants you wish to grow. Simple additional plantings of no more than two colours should be used to pick out one or more of the flowering climbers or shrubs that form the main structure.

Many of the spring-flowering climbers are yellow and blue. For the underplanting I would propose the subtle pale cream of *Alyssum saxatile* 'Citrinum' contrasted with the deep yellows of some of the Darwin hybrid tulips. Of the blue-flowering spring plants, few are lovelier than the sky-coloured forget-me-nots (*Myosotis scorpioides* or *M. sylvatica*) and the deep, bright blue of some *Iris reticulata* cultivars.

Pinks and reds begin to take over as the season develops (although white also becomes increasingly important). Among the first clematis to flower are the blue and pink forms of *Clematis macropetala*, followed by white and pink forms of *C. montana*. The large-flowered cultivars of *C. montana* bloom later in the summer and will mingle beautifully with red, pink and white roses. Juxtaposing clematis with roses like this has been a popular gardening ploy since the very first clematis for gardens were grown in the sixteenth century.

For a red scheme, try combining rose cultivars 'Ena Harkness' and 'Parkdirektor Riggers' with clematis 'Ernest Markham' and 'Madame Julia Correvon'. For pink, the roses 'Albertine' or 'Dorothy Perkins' go well with the clematis

'Nelly Moser'. If you want all white, try the roses 'Sanders' White' or 'Alberic Barbier' with the clematis 'Marie Boisselot' or 'Miss Bateman'.

Autumn is the season of warm orangey reds and yellows, whose gradations indicate various stages of glorious decay. In the vertical garden the most stunning displays are those of virginia creeper (*Parthenocissus quinquefolia*), Boston ivy (*P. tricuspidata* 'Veitchii') and the related *P. henryana*, whose dark green leaves, variegated with white and pink in summer, turn dark crimson-red.

The grapevine also takes on warm tints at this time of year. Particularly spectacular are *Vitis* 'Brant', *V. coignetiae* and *V. vinifera* 'Purpurea'. The latter is a wonderful foil for the late-flowering yellow clematis, *C. tangutica*. Autumn fruits add to the season's fiery regalia. Pyracantha, holly, *Rosa rugosa*, barberries and cotoneaster all have orange or red hips and berries that brighten the shortening days.

Creating a seasonal succession of colour is one

BELOW Clematis *'Ernest Markham'*, *one of the large-flowered cultivars that starts to bloom in mid-summer, has creamy-coloured stamens that associate very well with the variegated leaves of the* ivy, Hedera helix *'Goldheart'*. *The piece of mesh, which provides support for the clematis, could easily be hidden by a wall shrub, such as a white abutilon, to complete the composition.*

approach to garden planning: as one array of flowers fades, another of different hue – as in a relay race – takes up the baton. However, as an alternative, you may choose to devote all or part of your garden to a strictly limited spectrum. A pink and white garden, for example, offers plenty of scope. You can plan one that will be at its best in late spring and early summer but leave a lingering reminder during autumn and winter. For winter colour near the front door of the house, a pleasing effect can be achieved with *Viburnum* × *bodnantense* 'Dawn' under-planted with white *Cyclamen hederifolium* 'Album'. White *Clematis armandii* or pink *C. montana* 'Elizabeth' can be grown up a trellis or wall for colour in the early spring; the sweetly scented perpetual-flowering pink rose 'New Dawn' is excellent for colour throughout the summer; and a pot of white Headbourne Hybrid agapanthus will cheer up the late summer and early autumn.

Simple, natural-looking schemes such as these are usually more pleasing than more complex designs, which tend to look over-fussy and over-planted. Above all, you should be wary of introducing striking contrasts which could easily become tiring if overindulged. Handled in a controlled manner, contrast can look arresting and lend depth and relief to a design. For example, the purple *Solanum crispum* 'Glasnevin' flowering with the bright orange trumpets of *Campsis radicans* can be very exciting in late summer. Earlier in the year the pineapple-scented yellow *Cytisus battandierii* would give a slight shock to the senses grown with the repeat-flowering pink rose 'Galway Bay' – and even on its own will stimulate comment. Never overdo the contrast – unless you have a very good eye for colour, experiments can go wrong and spoil an otherwise wonderful effect. The smaller the plot, the greater the need for a light touch in the planting.

CENTRE *This is a garden in which the planting has been coordinated for spectacular interest in early summer, the climbers and border plants making a monochromatic alliance of pale lilacs and purples. The plants that compose this corner are* Clematis 'Nelly Moser', Centaurea montana *and chives that have been allowed to flower. The aquilegias are just beginning to fade, and tall lilies have yet to reveal themselves.*

ABOVE *An example of portable colour that harmonizes with its surroundings. Bright pink pelargoniums in a clay pot by the front door of a house painted soft pink make a positive statement to visitors and passers-by.*

THE ART OF SECLUSION

To create a garden is to make a piece of land your own. However small it is, you can relax here and feel at ease. One of the first considerations when planning the design is to ensure that the plot has the degree of privacy or protection you require. It may be overlooked by a host of other houses and, short of transforming the garden into a forest, you will never succeed in screening yourself from prying eyes. However, with some careful thought and planting you may be able to protect yourself from the worst visual intrusions and create an adequate sense of seclusion.

Even if you are in the fortunate position of not being overlooked at all, a very open garden may make you feel no less vulnerable and exposed. Creating some more private areas within your garden will dispel this feeling.

Start off by drawing a rough plan of the garden and the surrounding buildings and open spaces. Then take a slow walk around your plot and into the centre, making notes of the open spaces and the gaps, the viewpoints and the features within and beyond the garden that you would wish to incorporate into the design. Note the incidence of light, areas that are obscured by a building or existing tree, and any source of noise. Then, go into the house and make similar notes from each window. You will now be ready to decide where you need to erect screens to protect your patch and make the first steps toward exploiting the full possibilities of vertical gardening.

The first consideration must be the shell of the garden. This protects it and you from the outside world and defines the space inside. The boundaries need careful thought as mistakes early on may be difficult to reverse later. They must be functional, purposeful and interesting, the space they enclose well-proportioned and related to the human scale – intimate yet not claustrophobic. Success with the perimeters will normally lead to success with the interior space. While planning the garden enclosure, you should also look at the opportunities to create openings which offer views of the world beyond. This combines surprise and secrecy with invitation and spaciousness – further elements essential in a successful design.

The material of the enclosure should first of all be functional. What purpose does it need to fulfil? It may need to be very solid to obliterate a

LEFT *A solid brick wall, unadorned, provides seclusion but can look harsh and unfriendly, however mellow the bricks. The solution is a treatment such as this. Sculptures peep through the large-leaved, slightly tender ivy –* Hedera canariensis *– that grows in the wall's protection. The ivy has been trimmed to a carefully determined height to reveal a section of brickwork. Roses and clematis hang over from the other side – an effect that can sometimes be contrived if you have a cooperative neighbour.*

FAR LEFT *Even when not designed for sitting, an open, plant-covered arbour will help to create seclusion by adding a sense of complexity and volume to the space the garden occupies. This trellised arbour (in the secret garden at Tyninghame, Scotland) protects an old weathered statue. Roses have been planted at each corner to cloak the pillars and soften the structural form. All around the base is a row of lavender, which bars the entry and emphasizes the space within a space.*

view or keep out sounds or intruders. Brick would be the obvious choice if it weren't for the considerable cost of building a solid wall with good foundations. However, you may decide that the investment is worthwhile; or that, with patience and some effort, you can dig the foundations yourself and find second-hand bricks from specialist suppliers or in architectural salvage yards. The outlay may be well worth considering if it enhances your environment and adds to the value of your property.

What are the alternatives to brick? A solid fence could have the right visual effect. Although fences are usually made to disappear, their design possibilities are multiple, and they can be turned into a feature that suits the style of the house. You could choose a battened slat fence or interwoven panels. Neither will have the mellow feel of a brick wall; moreover, they are fairly expensive and, unless regularly maintained, deteriorate with age, rather than acquire patina. Cheaper wattle or woven fences can only be considered as temporary structures.

A hedge, which would give substance and distinction to the garden, would take at least ten years to grow to a reasonable size. Suitable evergreen species could include the fast-growing Leyland cypress (× *Cupressocyparis leylandii*); *Thuja occidentalis*, which is slower growing; yew, so long as there is no livestock to be poisoned by the foliage or berries; holly, which is delightful but which can be difficult to prune; and either the Portuguese laurel (*Prunus lusitanica*) or the cherry laurel (*P. laurocerasus*). The deciduous beech and hornbeam give a slightly less substantial effect but their colour is both fresh in the spring and rich through the autumn and winter: not until spring do the leaves fall. Hedges are very much cheaper than walls but compete with other plants for nutrients, water and light, take up more space and need regular care. (See also pages 42–47.)

An enclosure may be used simply to define a boundary without obscuring the scene beyond. A trellis fence, or one made of sturdy uprights linked with chains or rope, and clothed with climbers, would seclude the garden from the outside world, forming a physical barrier without entirely being a visual one. Alternatively, a low, informal flowering hedge could be equally effective.

Having defined the framework of your garden, you may choose to create additional secluded areas within that space. A small arbour or open summer house or pergola will provide the privacy for sitting and enjoying your garden without being observed or disturbed. Plan the structure so that the main openings are toward the sunshine at the time of day when you are most likely to be there, or toward the prettiest views. The view toward the house may well be the ideal focal point for your opening: the house will serve as an admirable backcloth provided that you have clad it with good climbers, some well-planted window boxes and, perhaps, some pots either side of the door. Plants grown around the arbour or summer house give an added opportunity for imaginative and fragrant vertical gardening.

Changing the levels in the garden will not only give a greater illusion of space but will also create areas of the garden that are more sheltered than others. For example, a space big enough to take a table and chairs in the sunniest corner of the garden can be excavated to a foot or two (30–60cm), the excavated material being used to raise the surrounding level. Once the corner has been paved, a small retaining wall built and the area planted with small herbs or alpines, you would be surprised how set apart from the rest of the garden it can feel. Added privacy can be achieved by erecting a light pergola over the sitting area and covering it with climbers. (See also pages 80–87.)

LEFT *In this highly secluded water garden, a barrier of bamboo creates the effect of a forest clearing – the fence behind is totally hidden. On the opposite side of the pool, purple-leaved hazel performs a similar function. A group of coneflowers (*Rudbeckia*) provides a yellow colour focus. Black-painted wrought-iron seats and matching table invite the visitor to sit and relax in this oasis.*

BELOW *Narrowing the entrance to one part of the garden and changing its paving material (or its level) can subtly delineate a space dedicated to relaxation. In this case the seating area, in the sunniest part of the patio, is defined by a brick platform. Terracotta lions at the entrance, and an architectural screen topped by a white finial, help to reinforce this sense of enclosure.*

BELOW *A simple wrought-iron gate makes a transparent barrier between two garden areas on either side of a wall, secluding one from the other. The white clematis, weaving* *through the ironwork, breaks the symmetry of the arch and deliberately obscures the view. The enclosed mood is heightened by an obvious focus – an oil jar filled with pelargoniums.*

RIGHT *This old cloistered court, providing a quiet seating area, has begun to acquire the patina of age and, with it, a romantic aura. The profuse flowers and wild straggliness of the honeysuckle contribute to the feel of a secret place which time has passed by.*

LEFT *Corridors between walls of foliage can be used to make the garden more mysterious, heightening the mood of privacy. Here the muted colours add much to the serenity of the scene. Cream hollyhocks on the left,* Macleaya cordata *(about to bloom, on the right) and marguerites have been planted at the verge of the narrow path so that they will obscure the view as they grow, arousing the visitor's curiosity about what might lie beyond. Pleached limes above the path are just ready for summer pruning.*

BELOW *Shrub roses on a garden wall give privacy from passers-by, while providing them with a superb display all summer. Pink pompoms of* Rosa *'Raubritter' intermingle with the single open flowers of the thorny* R. × paulii. *Both are slightly scented.*

WALLS & BOUNDARIES

Walls, fences and hedges – including the walls of the house themselves – are important components of the garden, providing privacy and shelter and helping to articulate the design. An imaginative choice of climbing or hanging plants can transform blank vertical surfaces into colour, texture and fragrance – and even a source of fresh home-grown fruit.

HEDGES

There is something particularly satisfying and restful in the sight of a well-kept, strong hedge. Since the beginning of garden making, hedges have been planted, trimmed and cared for. They are a part of gardening tradition and anyone who can grow a hedge should do so.

Hedges can be formal or informal, evergreen or deciduous, tall or low. Depending on the site and climate, there will always be a suitable species to choose. Your decision as to which species to plant will also be governed by the time you feel you can wait to see it reach a reasonable height – bearing in mind too the time you have available for maintenance. A fast-growing hedge will need two or even three cuts a year to keep it looking good; a slower-growing species will only require one annual cut.

A hedge will, of course, take longer to produce an effect than a wall or a fence, and you should therefore consider some kind of temporary screening until the hedge is tall enough to block out unwanted views or winds. I once planted a beech hedge in an apse at the end of a planned vista. The beechlings were grown from seed and were no more than a foot (30cm) high when they were planted out. They did not close the vista, and neither did they hide from sight an offensive heap of tyres in the adjacent farmyard. As an interim screen I erected a light trellis covered with a green hessian. As well as being inexpensive, this sort of structure has the advantage of having a limited life: by the time the beech needed more space and light the hessian had deteriorated, leaving only the trellis which then served as a trimming guide. Trellis was commonly used in this way in the eighteenth century to define newly planted hedges, giving impact until the plant filled the space allocated.

It is important to plan the hedge before planting it. First, you must decide on its purpose – whether, for example, it is to be a screen, a backdrop to a garden feature (such as a statue, container, or flower or shrub border), or a barrier on the boundaries of the garden. Are you planting the hedge in the right position? Is there enough space for the top and roots of the hedge to develop over the years? Hedging plants may be a spindly 2 feet (60cm) high when you put them in the ground but could eventually reach up to 6 or 8 feet (1.8–2.4m), spreading to 2 or 3 feet (60–90cm) in width. Will there be space then to navigate round the whole hedge so that you can trim it in comfort? A cramped hedge is difficult to look after and will give little satisfaction. If the garden is very small it follows that only low-growing hedges will be suitable.

RIGHT *Forsythia is an ideal shrub for making a flowering hedge. It blooms in early spring, before the leaves appear, on the old wood. Any trimming should be done immediately after the flowers have faded: cut out the dead wood and, if necessary, thin out overcrowded branches.*

RIGHT *Fronting this country house is a spectacular hedge of* Rosa rugosa *whose hips look as attractive in the autumn as the flowers do in early summer. This rose is admirable for smaller gardens because its compact root system does not compete excessively with those of nearby plants for water and nutrients. It requires only light trimming in late winter or early spring and flowers on the current season's growth.*

RIGHT *Though yew makes a relatively slow-growing hedge, it rewards patient gardeners by providing an ideal subject for topiary. This topiary garden at Levens Hall, Cumbria, was probably planted around 1700, making it one of the oldest in the world. The rich sculptural pattern is made all the more interesting by the use of contrasting green and yellow-leaved forms.*

Whatever species you decide to grow, the ground must be well prepared for planting. Weed it thoroughly and incorporate as much organic material as possible into well-dug root holes. These should be large enough to accommodate the roots when they are completely spread out. It is useful to add some pre-emergence herbicide, such as simazine, to the soil you use to pack around the roots and to scatter a well-balanced, slow-release fertilizer over the top of the soil at the base of each plant.

To save time when planting, it is sensible to dig and fill as follows: take the soil from the first hole to the last hole; use the soil from the second hole to fill round the roots of the first plant; use the soil from the third hole to fill the second; and so on to the end. Water in the plants thoroughly after planting to ensure that there are no air pockets left around the roots.

Careful training and weeding in the early years is essential for the establishment of a good hedge. Allow the leader of each plant to grow until it has reached the desired height, and cut the laterals back by two thirds in the first and second years to build up a strong framework. As the hedge begins to fill out, trim it so that it is slightly wider at the base to enable maximum light penetration. A slight batter also prevents snow from sitting on the top and breaking the branches.

Personally, I find the task of clipping hedges very satisfying. From a straggly unkempt embarrassment, the hedge is quickly transformed into a neat and crisp shape. Electric hedge cutters are useful for trimming small-leaved species such as box and privet, and some conifers — and, obviously, for tackling long stretches of hedge. However, a better finish is achieved with hand shears. Cutting will be easier if you work from the bottom up so that the clippings can fall to the ground unimpeded. Large-leaf species of hedging plant such as Portuguese and cherry laurels must be cut with secateurs.

Informal hedges need less maintenance. Dead branches need to be cut out each year and the occasional overgrown branch will need cutting right down to keep the hedge in shape as well as to encourage new branches and maintain vigour. Camellias, roses, osmanthus and lilac can all be trimmed when the shrub is in flower and the cut branches used in the house for decoration. Other shrubs that flower mainly on the previous year's growth, such as *Berberis × stenophylla*, *Buddleja alternifolia* and *Spiraea* 'Arguta' should be pruned immediately after flowering; those that flower on the current season's growth, such as fuchsias and shrubby potentillas, can be pruned in early spring.

If you have inherited an old and neglected hedge, it is often possible to rejuvenate it by careful and drastic pruning. It is best to do this over two growing seasons. In the first year, lightly trim one side and cut the other as far back to the central leader as possible; cut the other side the following year.

Yew and hornbeam are my own favourite hedging plants. They are among the traditional species that have been used to make attractive divisions within the garden for centuries. They are good growers, neither too fast nor too slow, they make solid barriers and they require only one clip a year.

Other evergreens suitable for hedging include: box (alas, rarely grown as a big hedge these days because of its slow growth); the large-leaved Portuguese laurel (*Prunus lusitanica*) and cherry laurel (*P. laurocerasus*); sweet bay (*Laurus nobilis*); the many forms of the hollies *Ilex aquifolium* and *Ilex × altaclerensis*; and, for the colder climates of northern America, *I. crenata* or *I. × meserveae* and its cultivars.

Evergreens are, as a rule, less hardy than deciduous trees but there are forms within species that are markedly hardier than others. It is a shame that breeders do not make more

LEFT *The combination of evergreen yew and deciduous beech makes a good backdrop for the boldly coloured scheme of tulips and forget-me-nots. Both trees, once established, need to be trimmed back hard in mid-summer and again, lightly, in late autumn. The yew's solid even colour provides a counterpoint to the broad, light green leaves of the beech all summer, and makes a fine background for boldly coloured annuals. In the autumn, the beech will turn coppery brown against the yew's unchanging green.*

selections for hardiness, as it is so disappointing to have a hedge decimated by a harsh winter. In a nursery in Holland, which I visited after one severe winter, I observed, within the rows, significant differences in hardiness among yew trees (*Taxus baccata*). The stand of the hybrid *T. × media* 'Hicksii' was the only one without any signs of damage.

Other hardy hedge plants that will generally come through a cold winter unscathed are western red cedar (*Thuja plicata*); arborvitae (*T. occidentalis*) and their cultivars; the western hemlock (*T. heterophylla*) and the less commonly used eastern hemlock (*Tsuga canadensis*); *Chamaecyparis lawsoniana*; and the very quick-growing × *Cupressocyparis leylandii*. It is a pity that this last-mentioned somewhat vulgar cyprus hybrid is the only one to be really robust: anyone blessed with a milder climate should grow the more elegant *Cupressus sempervirens* which can be clipped to form a barrier as little as 10 inches (25cm) in width.

For less favoured areas, where winter temperatures drop very low and for prolonged periods, it is better to choose deciduous species. Quickthorn, beech or hornbeam (which is better suited to acid soils), *Berberis thunbergii* and *Corylus avellana* are dependable choices. The deciduous *Euonymus alatus* 'Compactus' is a good substitute for the evergreen *Euonymus japonica*, *Elaeagnus angustifolia* for *E. pungens maculata* and *Myrica pensylvanica* for

RIGHT *This tapestry hedge was created by planting alternate trees of the green-leaved and copper-leaved types of beech. The colours interweave at random to make a pleasing barrier that will never look the same two years running.*

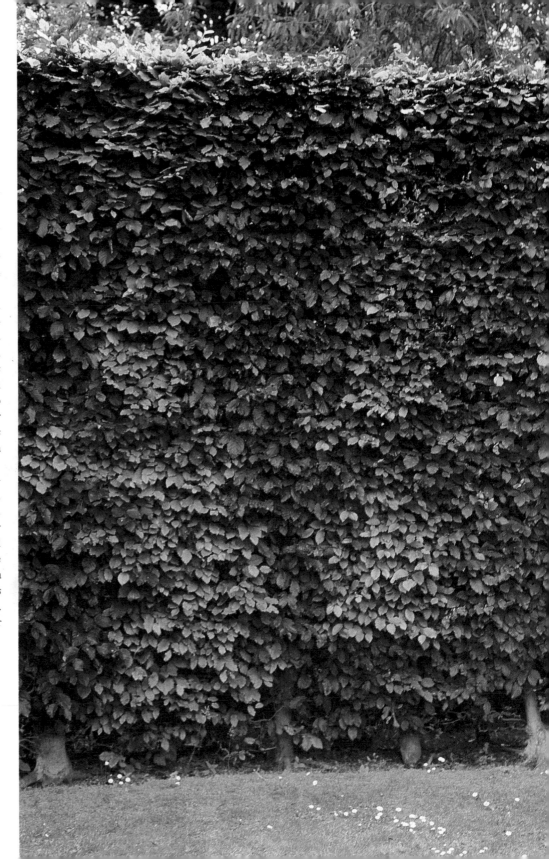

M. californica. Among the *Prunus* species are three that are particularly successful when grown as hedges: *P. cerasifera, P. × cistena* and *P. nigra.* Lots of small white flowers crowd the twigs of all three species in the early spring if they are pruned immediately after flowering.

Finally, you must remember that hedges take a lot of nutrients and water from the ground and block out light on at least one side – so they will compete with any plant growing nearby. This means that borders, or even specimen shrubs and trees, need to be planted far enough away from the hedge to ensure that all will thrive. A path of about 3 feet (90cm) is necessary to separate a hedge from a herbaceous border. Shrubs and trees need planting further from the hedge, depending on their ultimate size.

For planting at the base of a hedge there are numerous small species that will relish the dry conditions. On the sunny side bulbs such as tulips, daffodils, crocus, scillas and *Iris reticulata* are a good choice, provided that they are dressed with a balanced fertilizer annually. Also suitable for dry soil are annuals such as helichrysum, mesembryanthemum, nasturtium and *Phlox drummondii*, and some perennials such as aubrieta, *Campanula portenschlagiana*, day lilies, bearded irises and catmint. On the shady side periwinkle, ivies, *Hypericum calycinum*, some ferns, primroses and polyanthus, violas, monkshood and hostas are among the most suitable plants.

LEFT *This mixed hedge combines two evergreens to make a formal pattern. The variegated holly makes a striking contrast to the uniform green of the yew. Hedges are best trimmed from the base upward so that the cut branches can fall to the ground without being obstructed: this is particularly important with sharp-leaved species such as holly which can be very painful to deal with.*

'Walls should only have such coverings that neither confuse the design nor damage the structure.' This is the recommendation given by Gertrude Jekyll and Christopher Hussey in a chapter entitled 'Over growth' in *Garden Ornaments*, their great tome published in 1918.

As a student I once expressed the view that plants were grown on buildings simply to hide bad architecture. How wrong-headed this was! I have since mellowed and learned the value of warm walls for growing some of the delightful species that are on the borderline of hardiness.

Of course, it is true that a plain house can be greatly improved by a covering of wall shrubs and climbers. Beautiful architecture can be enhanced in the same way. However, regardless of the architectural merits of the house, great care must go into the selection of suitable plants that will complement its character and not do structural damage.

Most houses have at least two or three elevations, if not four, each providing different growing conditions and thus the opportunity to plant numerous different species. At least one side of the house will be more exposed to the prevailing winds than the others and should only be planted with the more robust species that can survive the dessicating effects of cold winter blasts.

Remember, too, that the soil at the bottom of a wall is always drier than that further from the house, though the side that receives the least sun will often be more damp than the rest. You will need to be sure that you can gain access with a hose if you are planning to plant particularly thirsty species.

The next point to bear in mind is the general habit of the plant in relation to the site you have chosen. Do you need a plant that will grow upward, or one that will grow across a wall, or both? Do you want a deciduous plant or an evergreen? Are you prepared to climb ladders to clip and train a fast-growing plant? Can ties be inserted into the wall easily, or would a self-supporting plant be preferable?

Great care, too, should be taken to prevent vigorous species from clogging up gutters and drainpipes or getting under roof tiles. Plants should frame views through windows, not obscure them. They should greet you warmly at the door, not bar the entry. Control is therefore of the essence.

You must prepare the site thoroughly if your chosen specimen is to have a chance of establishing itself and growing healthily. More than anywhere else in the garden, the soil immediately around the house is likely to be poor, particularly on a new site where the foundation trenches will be full of builder's debris which will never make a good growing medium. This should be removed and replaced with good topsoil from another area of the garden or a proprietary growing compost – to which should be added some slow-release nutrient. Be careful to ensure that the bed does not bridge the damp proof course and render it ineffective.

Of all the climbers that grace the walls of town and country houses, wisteria is one of the most popular and intriguing. Even in winter, bare of flowers and leaves, its twisted ancient-looking stems have a peculiar charm. However, it is a particularly vigorous plant and has been known, particularly after a drought and on clayey soil, to damage the foundations. On the other hand, many is the country house that has supported a wisteria for nearly a century without suffering any damage, the plant developing year by year, and filling the whole house with delicious scent in the early summer.

Hydrangea petiolaris is another splendid wall shrub with the merit of being happy on a shady wall. It is a vigorous, self-clinging species which

LEFT *Under the eaves of a cottage, variegated ivy meeting* Clematis *'Comtesse de Bouchaud' in a classic contrast frames an arch-shaped area of honey-coloured stone wall. A hoop of iron supplies a support for the clematis leaf-stalks to cling to. Visible in the bottom right-hand corner is* Campanula garganica, *with blue, star-shaped flowers; its seedlings will take root in unlikely crannies.*

ABOVE *This window has been planned for all-year interest. The blue-painted window box contrasts effectively with showy petunias. In autumn the deep overhang of Boston ivy (*Parthenocissus tricuspidata*) will turn a delicious dark crimson and produce waxy dark blue fruit. Notable here is the use of a few white petunias to offset all that colour – a trick none the less effective for its familiarity.*

CENTRE *A dark crinkle-leaved ivy mingles with the yellow-green leaves of a wisteria in high summer. A single pot of bright red pelargoniums on the left echoes the full window box in the centre of the picture. Both draw the eye upward to take in the shape of the windows and the Victorian gas lamp projecting from the house wall.*

RIGHT *The shady entrance to this cottage is brightened by* Campanula portenschlagiana: *in a more favourable position this plant can become invasive, and seedlings need relentless weeding out. The red rose on the sunniest side, 'Danse du Feu', is past its best, whereas the flowers in the shade are noticeably smaller, sparser and later to bloom. Ivy and ferns form the backcloth to the changing colour.*

BELOW *A virginia creeper has taken hold of this house, covering the shutters, filling the gutters and lifting the roof tiles. This kind of overgrowth can occur within a season.*

will grow to 80 feet (25m) and, once established, flowers every year without fail in early summer. I once saw it flanking the great classical portico of a Kentish house, neatly clipped so as not to ruin the symmetry of the composition, convincing me that the plant complements fine architecture and is amenable to discipline.

A closely allied species, not grown often enough in my opinion, is *Schizophragma hydrangeoides*. This is somewhat less strong-growing, reaching 40 feet (12m); the great flower heads, up to 10 inches (25cm) across, consist of white bracts which appear in mid-summer. Like the hydrangea, it supports itself by aerial roots and tolerates shade, although flowering is most successful where there is more sun.

Both species are natives of Japan, as is *Nandina domestica* which – as its specific name suggests – is a plant associated with houses: in Japan just about every courtyard used to have one. It is an attractive evergreen whose young foliage unfurls in shades of crimson, copper and bronze in contrast with the mature green leaves, which turn bright crimson in the autumn. Long, frothy panicles of white flowers are followed, in warmer areas, by a crop of red berries. These are used in the south-west of France (around Pau) for Christmas decorations. The plant is widely grown throughout the southern USA and on the Pacific coast. It was introduced to the West in 1804 and for a long time was considered too tender to grow out of doors. The celebrated plantsman E.A. Bowles grew it against the walls of Myddelton House, near London, during the first half of this century. The shrub's chief enemy is cold wind and, so long as it is sheltered, it will flourish where frosts are infrequent. It likes a neutral to acid soil and dislikes alkalinity.

RIGHT *Relatively sparse planting on a house wall can be effective – especially if balanced by plenty of interest at ground level. On this corner, a rose rises from a bank of* Alchemilla mollis, *which tolerates such dry conditions. Later in the season, yellow pansies will brighten the base of the adjacent wall.*

Other tender species worth trying in areas where winter frosts are neither too hard nor too frequent include *Fremontodendron californicum*, which has deep butter-yellow, star-shaped flowers all summer. On a sunny wall the new wood stands a good chance of ripening before winter and therefore of withstanding the cold. Two other favourites are *Campsis radicans*, which has stunning orange-red trumpet-shaped flowers, and *Crinodendron hookerianum*, whose flowers are delicate, red and bell-shaped. There is also a rarer white-flowered crinodendron, *C. patagua*, which grows faster but is more tender.

Another native of Chile that likes a shady position sheltered from cold winds is *Berberidopsis corallina*. It thrives in an acid soil and flowers from early summer for three months or so, depending on the climate, with racemes of coral-coloured hanging bells which stand out well against the dark green shiny leaves.

All these slightly tender plants will appreciate being given a modicum of protection during the winter. The roots and lower stem should be wrapped in straw or covered with expanded polystyrene granules held down with black polythene (perforated for drainage). This way, if the upper part of the plant does suffer frost damage and has to be cut back to the stem, growth may start again from the base after a little feeding and patience. My motto is never to give up a plant for dead until it has failed to show signs of life the following season!

Finally, I like to have some winter-flowering plants around the house to cheer me on through the cold weather. These are best grown on a wall shaded from the morning sun, to avoid scorching the frozen blossoms. The two that spring to mind are *Jasminum nudiflorum*, the hardiest of the jasmines, which never fails to delight with its delicate, yellow flowers, and *Chimonanthus praecox*, which has the most fragrant, palest greeny-yellow flowers even in deepest winter.

RIGHT *Twin windows within pointed arches are luxuriantly embellished with* Hydrangea petiolaris. *This deciduous climber requires no support and does well on a shady wall. It needs plenty of moisture and good drainage. Though shy to flower in the early years, it will bloom profusely every summer once established.*

RIGHT *This old wooden door to an outbuilding is framed by a collection of red, pink and yellow roses, arching asymmetrically. With repeated pruning and deadheading, many climbing roses can be encouraged to flower all summer.*

LEFT *The clean lines of a neo-Gothic window are emphasized by the crisp old rose 'Madame Alfred Carrière', one of the most popular of all white climbers. Its double flowers are sweetly fragrant.*

RIGHT *The graceful racemes of* Wisteria sinensis *droop around the porch of a classical town house, their colour and scent offering a feast for the senses. The flowers on wisteria open progressively from the stem to the tip, so that the grape-like clusters become fuller and more fragrant over a period of several days. Pruning should be carried out in mid-summer so that the new growth has ample time to mature before winter, when it should be shortened again.*

LEFT *Carefully trimmed to an H shape around the windows,* Vitis coignetiae *spreads its autumn foliage over the rear brick wall of a house. Along the foot of the wall is a low raised bed filled with groundcover plants. A pot plant precisely placed beneath the window adds a touch of formality to this otherwise relaxed design.*

CENTRE *Wisteria is often used in isolation. This is a more original treatment, in which its curtain of fragrant spring flowers contrasts with walls of small-flowered begonia, supported by a balustrade.*

WALLS OF SCENT

Fragrance in the garden can come as a real bonus and should be planned for accordingly. Everyone has their own interpretation of smells and their impact and value, and a plant that may seem sickly or slightly acrid to one person may give unexpected pleasure to another. It is best, therefore, to familiarize yourself with the scents of a variety of plants in a nursery, or other people's gardens, so as to select those that most appeal to you.

The greater the variety of fragrant plants you are able to grow in your garden, the more they will contribute to the "genius of the place". Jason Hill wrote in *The Curious Gardener* (1932) that scented plants constitute an "invisible garden": fragrance adds a dimension that is not detectable to the eye. However, the presence of butterflies and bees around a plant is often a good indication of scent.

Fragrant plants are particularly associated with gardens for the blind but are, alas, too rarely included in other schemes. After all, spring is not just a matter of daffodils, primroses and birdsong. For me spring has really arrived when I have caught that crisp, fresh smell of exciting things to come, the scent of sun-warmed soil and new foliage which is especially distinct in temperate climates. Further south it is the characteristic smells of summer that are most marked: a heady air, laden with the aromas of rosemary, thyme, lavender and myrtle wafting around among the sound of crickets. Autumn's essence is a mixture of bonfire smells and the distinctive

odours of rotting leaves. Winter offers the somewhat less tangible scent of frost on earth and foliage, and the distinctive nutmeg fragrance of flowering viburnum.

The idea of a wall of scent conjures up images of a great barrage of fragrance. This could, indeed, be achieved by careful plant selection. But even more delightful, perhaps, would be a succession of subtle fragrances developing in tandem with the changing shades and colours of the garden. In planning for this, it makes sense to site your scented plants in positions where you are most likely to enjoy them – near the front door, around the windows of the house or alongside a much-frequented path. Alternatively, a completely enclosed scented garden could be created using hedges of fragrant species, such as sweet-smelling roses or sweet peas, growing through trelliswork obelisks – a retreat that would soothe the spirit and delight the senses.

This is no new idea. In 1881 Frances Jane Hope, an enthusiastic amateur who lived and gardened near Edinburgh and contributed regularly to the *Gardeners' Chronicle*, wrote a charming piece on pleached alleys in which she recommended planting four different poplars – balsam (*Populus balsamifera*), aspen (*P. tremula*), Italian or Lombardy poplar (*P. nigra* 'Italica') and abele or white poplar (*P. alba*) – to make a fragrant winter alley that would also serve as "the most pleasant resort on a close summer's day".

ABOVE *A beautifully crafted bench is the perfect place to sit and enjoy the strong scent of the rose named after the great flower arranger, Constance Spry. A very vigorous shrub or pillar rose, growing up to 8 feet (2.5m) in height, it needs careful training and tying in. 'Constance Spry' produces large double pink flowers in midsummer. Although not a repeat-flowering rose, it has attractive deep green foliage.*

LEFT *At the base of this stone pier clad in the unscented rose 'American Pillar', fragrance comes from a clump of lavender. Both the flowers and leaves are aromatic. To make a lavender hedge you should choose a sunny spot with a light soil, and space individual plants about 1 foot (30cm) apart.*

The balsam poplar has a particularly pungent smell when in bud in early spring. I caught it once when cycling along a country lane where this fast-growing species had been used as a windbreak for an orchard. It was so striking that I had to cycle up and down the road several times to satisfy my olfactory senses to the full.

Jane Hope also described a summer alley in which honeysuckle and roses were mingled – "the orthodox Shakesperian roses and lush woodbine", as she puts it. There are three winter-flowering honeysuckles that would qualify as being lush and sweetly scented: *Lonicera fragrantissima*, *L. standishii* and their hybrid *L. × purpusii*. The best of the summer-flowering species are the evergreen *L. japonica* 'Halliana' and the deciduous *L. caprifolium* which both flower early. They are succeeded by *L. etrusca*, a vigorous semi-evergreen, and *L. × americana* which has been in cultivation in Europe since 1730 and is reputed to grow wild in North America. The European common woodbine, *L. periclymenum*, has two selected forms: 'Belgica', also known as 'Early Dutch', and the later-flowering 'Serotina'. Being native to hedge-rows and woodlands, honeysuckles like their roots to be in shade.

There is an even wider selection of sweetly scented roses. My own personal favourites are the species roses and old-fashioned cultivars. Recent introductions have large blowsy flowers at the expense of much of their scent. The colours are also much less subtle and when you grow old and new cultivars side by side you realize how vulgar the modern ones are. However, this is a question of taste. Other factors in deciding which roses to grow will depend on availability and on how you wish to grow them. Some are more suited for growing against walls, both sunny and shady, some are excellent for pergolas and summer houses, while others make splendid scented hedges. In the latter category I would mention just one, *Rosa rubiginosa*, which is notable for the scent not of its flowers but of its leaves; this is particularly pungent after rain. Its branches can be clipped quite hard as the flowers are not the main reason for including *R. rubiginosa* in the garden.

Many other sweet-smelling species make suitable informal hedges, particularly *Philadelphus microphyllus*, which has large flowers and the virtue of not growing much more than 4 feet (1.2m) tall. The hardy double-flowered *Syringa vulgaris* cultivars and hawthorn will both make large hedges if they are given their head and allowed to flower. For best results you should either prune the hedge back hard every second year and allow it to flower in the alternate years; or trim half of the new growth every year, allowing the other half to grow on and flower.

LEFT *The popular 'New Dawn' rose spreads its charming flowers around a beautiful niche in an old stone wall. This plant flowers freely, but its sweet scent is detectable even when there is only a small number of blooms on display.*

FAR LEFT *Two highly scented Bourbon climbers meet above a doorway in a brick perimeter wall. The rose on the left is the old favourite 'Zéphirine Drouhin', introduced in 1868; on the right is one of her sports, 'Kathleen Harrop', which is not quite as vigorous as her parent. Sports, or mutants, occur when a rose raised from seed has different characteristics to the parent – often reverting to an older form. These two roses are ideal for growing together, as they will flower freely and repeatedly from midsummer on.*

BELOW *The honeysuckle, or woodbine, has traditionally provided a sweet scent in the cottage garden. It needs support to grow up a wall. It will show itself at its best climbing through a small tree, a trellis or a pergola. This is the early Dutch honeysuckle, Lonicera periclymenum 'Belgica', which blooms in late spring or early summer.*

A hedge of *Thuja plicata* smells of crushed orange peel. Box has its own distinctive smell, which is not appreciated by everyone. In warmer climates bay makes a dense attractive evergreen hedge which, if cut back by the frost, usually comes back with great vigour during the following season.

Low hedges can be composed of lavender, rosemary and santolina which will stand clipping and fill the air with fragrance. Thymes (creeping, lemon and woolly), mints of all descriptions, and dianthus cultivars (border pinks) such as 'Mrs Sinkins', which has the evocative scent of nutmeg, all do well at the base of walls where it is often too dry for many other plants. Walls also provide shelter and warmth for tender species native to the warmer frost-free climates, such as *Cytisus battandieri, Myrtus communis, Aloysia citriodora, Jasminum officinale* and *Trachelospermum asiaticum*. By an open window in the summer, any of these will fill the room with scent and intrigue visitors.

BELOW *Sweet peas (*Lathyrus odoratus*) will cover a wall or fence rapidly, soon reaching 7 feet (2m) or more. You can also grow them up a wigwam of canes or allow them to clamber up shrubs. Modern strains have been bred for their size and profuse flowering, and in the process some have lost the sweet scent that we associate with old cottage garden varieties. However, seed houses should be able to recommend strains notable for fragrance.*

EDIBLE WALLS

I always maintain that the seed of my love for horticulture was sown in my grandfather's garden when I was a child. There, I often pestered him with questions while he was hard at work preparing the beds for a new crop. What was he going to plant there, I would ask. Carrots. But, I protested, carrots were growing over *here* last year. My grandfather would then patiently explain the principles of crop rotation.

That garden, in which I received my first basic lessons in horticulture, was a typical French *potager*. It was enclosed by walls to protect it from the bitter winds which blow across the plain to the north-west of Paris. The house was positioned to the south of the garden so there were three sunny walls on which to grow fruit, including grapes, apples, pears and a cherry in a north-facing corner.

Not only were the walls used for fruit, but each bed was also surrounded by apple espaliers. These were at most 2 feet (60cm) high and made a most charming edge at all times of the year, flowering and cropping remarkably well, easy to prune and to pick. But they did require constant pruning to keep them at this height for, in those days, dwarfing rootstocks were unknown.

Nowadays we have dwarfing rootstocks for numerous varieties of apples, pears, cherries and plums. Although careful and regular training is still necessary to obtain a good crop, it is not the constant job it once was.

As many as ten different cultivars can be grown in a 30-foot (10m) run to create an edible wall that will always be changing as the blossoms burst open and the fruit develops through the year. The best approach is to plant cordons at an angle of 45° to the ground, spaced about 3 feet (90cm) apart, each supported by wire stretched between two posts. This provides a useful hedge within the garden to separate the flower garden from, say, the vegetable plot.

BELOW *The black branches of an espalier-trained pear tree make a dramatic winter effect against a white wall. Light-coloured walls reflect the sun in* *the summer, hastening the ripening of fruit – a necessity in colder climates. The twiggy branches need light pruning before the buds break in spring.*

Growing several different cultivars together will improve fertilization and therefore the chances of a good crop. No apple or pear is truly self-fertile: to achieve pollination, most require pollen to be transferred to their stigmas from the anthers of another, compatible strain.

Summer pruning should be carried out from mid to late summer to reduce lateral growth and let the light in. Winter pruning is necessary to shape the tree. With dwarf stock these pruning sessions are easy tasks. Spraying also becomes more manageable as you are able to reach all parts of the tree. Thinning and picking fruit are no longer the chore they once were and the crop will be plentiful with no wastage of fruits that in pre-dwarfstock days would be too high to pick.

The specific nutrient requirements of dwarf trees will depend on the type and condition of the soil they are planted in. Generally speaking, very fertile soils are not suitable for fruit growing as too much nitrogen encourages excessive growth at the expense of fruit. This can be counter-balanced with an application of potash, which encourages fruit bud formation. As a rule of thumb, you should incorporate the fruit trees into the general feeding programme of the garden, applying the necessary fertilizer in late winter or early spring. Pears succeed best on heavier (well-drained) soils, whereas apples are happier growing in light soils.

Good nurseries will supply already trained fruit trees on dwarfing, virus-free rootstocks. Many apple cultivars growing on rootstocks MM9 and MM106 are available, but it is advisable to avoid tip bearers and biennial bearers. Among the best for the quality of their fruit are dessert apples 'Discovery', 'James Grieve', 'Lord Lambourne', 'Sunset' and 'Tydeman's Late Orange'; and, among cooking apples, 'Reverend Wilks' and 'Lane's Prince Albert'.

Pears are grown on rootstocks Quince A or C. 'Merton Pride', 'Conference', 'Beurré Hardy'

and 'Doyenné du Comice' (if you have a warm, sunny wall) are among the most reliable.

Stone fruit trees are best trained into a fan shape by cutting back the vigorous central stem. Two new stems will then grow up either side; these should be partially cut back the following season and two further shoots each side allowed to grow. Repeat this exercise annually until the space is filled. Thereafter the only pruning required will be in the summer as for apples and pears. Suitable cultivars available are cherries (on dwarfing rootstock 'Colt') 'Stella', 'Merton Glory' and 'Van'; plum (on 'Pixie' stock) 'Victoria', and gages 'Early Transparent' and 'Late Transparent'. If any of these becomes over-vigorous it is possible to cut the roots.

Peaches, nectarines and apricots need a protected sunny wall and are well worth trying in warmer areas, if only because the fruit is particularly delicious when eaten straight from the tree. Those commonly available include peach 'Peregrine' on rootstock St Julian A, nectarines 'Lord Napier' and 'Early Rivers' and apricots 'Alfred' and 'Moorpark'.

Figs are more challenging to grow out of doors as they are not completely hardy, and will only fruit successfully if special care is taken to protect them from the cold. Fruit initiated during the growing season overwinters on the tree, ripening the following season. It is these unripe fruits that are vulnerable to frost. Free-standing trees can be packed up in straw for the winter. However, this is a time-consuming operation. A tree grown against a warm house wall is easier to protect with some wire mesh and straw, or bubble polythene, pulled over the top. Vigour is another problem: figs need severe root restriction if the tree is to be kept within bounds. A common method of achieving this is to plant the tree in a concrete-lined pit.

Grapes and Chinese gooseberries (*Actinidia chinensis* – the kiwifruit) are both vigorous climbers that will fruit on a warm sunny wall. They both need a long growing season that is free from frost – in the spring to avoid damage to young shoots and in the autumn when the maturing fruit is vulnerable. Pollination will be improved if each of the flowers is brushed in turn with a rabbit tail. Once established, Chinese gooseberry is easy to maintain: the only real task is to prune back the over-vigorous shoots and make sure that the fruit is not hidden from the sunlight it needs behind one of the plant's huge leaves.

The training and pruning of grape vines is slightly more complicated. Successful cropping relies on cutting back hard to delay growth until the risk of frost has passed, and restricting root growth to limit the amount of moisture received by the plant so as to hasten ripening of the fruit in the autumn. Large bunches of fruit may need thinning, and this should be done early on when the berries are about $\frac{1}{10}$ inch (2–3mm) in diameter, and again later when they are about pea-sized. There are several good varieties available including 'Royal Muscadine' (or 'Chasselas Doré'), 'Gamay Hâtive des Vosges', 'Scuppernong', 'Eden' and 'Strawberry'.

Many blackberries and other hybrid berries will thrive successfully against walls and wooden fences. They are easy to grow, particularly if they have plenty of moisture and a good sunny position. The best method of training is to ensure that, after the first year, the older fruit-bearing canes are kept separate from the current year's growth. One way to achieve this is to tie the young wood together in the centre of the wide fan formed by the old canes; then, as the old canes finish fruiting, cut them back and replace them with new shoots so that they receive as much light as possible. Among the best blackberry cultivars are 'Himalaya Giant' ('Theodor Reimers'), which is very thorny, and the parsley-leaved 'Oregon Thornless'.

CRACKS AND CRANNIES

There is a variety of *Saxifraga longifolia*, 'Tumbling Waters', that I dream to see growing *en masse* in a drystone wall. So far I have only seen it grown under glass, but even in the environment of a flower show its beauty is impressive: each plant sends out a great plume of white florets which curves gently downward like a snowy mountain waterfall. It is not an easy plant to grow well and I dare say I need to wait longer to see my dream come true of hundreds of massed plants flowing down a wall.

It is not, however, difficult to create a similar effect using the many small alpine plants that are easier to grow. Indeed, many require little attention once they have been planted in the right environment. Alpines grow in very well-drained soils in their native habitats and can be coaxed into the interstices of walls, within crumbling mortar or in specially constructed spaces in walls where the conditions are ideal.

In preparing a wall for planting it is necessary first to remove any self-seeded herbaceous or shrubby weeds, such as buddleia or sycamore. They may look very pretty but their roots can do substantial damage to brick or stonework.

Drystone walls, typical of the British Cotswolds region and New England, or old brick walls in which the mortar is deteriorating, are those best suited to planting. Where these do not exist you might consider building a retaining wall against a bank or slope. This will provide the right conditions for many delightful species.

Perhaps the most difficult task is locating a source of suitable stone. Limestone or sandstone are ideal but most types will do. If you can obtain flat-surfaced stones the wall will be easier to build. The stones should be slightly larger than bricks, with some larger still to act as anchors at several points along the wall.

Building a stone retaining wall should not be too difficult provided that you have a reasonably

ABOVE *In this vigorous clump of the Welsh poppy,* Meconopsis cambrica, *the early flowers have already matured to form slender oblong pods. Shortly these pods will burst and the seeds will find their way into yet more cracks in the old wall.*

straight eye and remember a few basic rules. The wall should not be built at a right angle to the ground but tilted back into the bank slightly to prevent the soil from washing away or falling out, and to ensure adequate drainage and maximum light. It helps to achieve a consistent angle along the length of the wall if you drive posts into the ground at each end and stretch a line between.

The angle of the slope will also be dictated by the depth of the stones you use, as each course needs to be set back approximately $\frac{1}{4}$inch (6mm) from the one below – which isn't always easy to judge if the stones are not very straight! As you complete each course make sure that you pack the soil behind the wall tightly to avoid subsequent settlement and sprinkle the top of the row with a $\frac{1}{2}$inch (12mm) layer of fine soil to make a bed for the next course of stones; I use a mixture of equal parts loam, peat, sand and chopped leafmould (or well-rotted manure, if available). It is important not to leave any air pockets so I always water the wall thoroughly at the end of each day as I am constructing it: this washes the soil down to fill any holes that might remain.

It is useful, also, to weight down the wall every four courses with some larger stones that you have put aside for this purpose. If the wall is to exceed 6 feet (1.8m) in height it will be safer if it is stepped half way up and the top half set back 1 to 2 feet (30–60cm). This also creates an additional planting space.

Plants can be inserted between the stones as the wall is being built. If you are planting in an existing wall, chisel out a space and use small pieces of rock or brick to wedge the plants in. It is best to use small pot-grown plants that already have a good root system and soil around them, so that they establish themselves quickly. Seed is more tricky as it will need the right germination and early growing conditions – enough water to germinate, followed by just enough moisture to

BELOW *A charming natural composition of the red valerian (*Centranthus ruber*) with the delicate lady fern (*Athyrium filix-femina*) adds distinction to a grey stone wall. The valerian will tolerate even the saline conditions of seaside gardens. It lives for a long time and seeds itself freely.*

RIGHT Anthemis cupaniana, *a native of Italy, likes to grow in well-drained soil, and is ideal for a sunny wall. Flowering freely through the summer, it can be propagated by division in autumn or early spring, or from seeds sown in the spring.*

FAR RIGHT, TOP Clematis × vedrariensis *'Highdown' is a near relation to C.* montana *but less vigorous. It grows well in shady wall crevices where the roots are protected from the sun.*

grow on without drying out altogether or suffering from a fungal condition known as "damping off". It is best to let the established plants seed themselves once the wall has settled down and developed an ecology of its own. Newly planted walls, particularly free-standing ones, will need to be kept moist during dry spells. Use a fine rose without too much water pressure or seeds and small plants will get washed away. Water retaining walls from behind.

There are some very easy plants that can be grown on a sunny, drier wall. Examples are the golden-flowered *Alyssum saxatile*; *Erigeron karvinskianus*, with its multitudes of daisy-like flowers; *Iberis sempervirens*, which has long racemes of white flowers; *Cerastium tomentosum*, justifiably named "snow in summer"; and *Sedum reflexum*, the yellow-flowered stonecrop. Plants that thrive better on damper, shadier walls include the spring-flowering *Aubrieta deltoidea*, available in various shades of red, pink, purple or white; *Centranthus ruber*, as attractive for its bushy habit as for its pink, red or white flowers; *Meconopsis cambrica*, which has yellow poppy-like flowers; *Campanula poscharskyana*, covered in lavender-blue flowers

LEFT Erigeron karvinskianus (mucronatus), *a member of the daisy family, is commonly known as fleabane. It is happiest on dry walls and forms a dense mat, flowering throughout summer and autumn. Once established it requires little attention, seeding itself with abandon.*

FAR RIGHT *Aubrieta deltoidea tumbles down a wall of attractively sloped stones. In a sunny position this evergreen, mat-forming alpine, native of southern Europe, is one of the first plants to flower in the spring, when it forms spectacular curtains of purple flowers. Aubrieta was discovered in 1690 by the French botanist Joseph Tournefort and named after Claude Aubriet, the botanical artist who accompanied him on the expedition.*

RIGHT *The red and green leaves of a sedum contrast distinctively with the large, irregular boulders of a stone wall. Interesting leaves like these make attractive shadows against stone.*

throughout the summer; and *Phlox subulata*, usually red to pink, but with a very attractive white form.

Other plants are more difficult and need special soils but once established can survive a long time and give a great deal of pleasure. *Lewisia cotyledon* has white flowers veined with pink in summer. It needs to be wedged firmly into a sunny crevice where its foliage will be protected from excessive water contact: like many members of the genus, it is vulnerable to root rot. Sprinkling some gravel around its neck will also help. There are a number of hybrids available with bright pink and orangey flowers, and these are more robust than their parents. The plants are not very long-lived but further specimens can be propagated by seed or, more easily, from cuttings. Seeds will germinate more freely and quickly if they are stored in the refrigerator for a month.

Ramonda myconi is another of my favourite rock plants. It is ideal for the damp or deeply shaded wall. The addition of a little peat to the growing medium will help to retain sufficient moisture for this thirsty plant – at the very first signs of droop it should be watered, and will generally recover provided that it is not subjected to prolonged drought. The plant has violet to purple flowers that closely resemble African violets and, like other members of the family Gesneriaceae, can be propagated most easily from leaf cuttings taken in summer as well as from careful division in spring. The seeds are minute and produce seedlings that need careful supervision or they tend to damp off.

I never grudge a little time for the more unusual plants, as they are always rewarding to nurture and add a little horticultural cachet to the garden. To find surprises among more common inhabitants of the garden is such a treat for visitors – it is a little like finding an unusual species growing in the wild.

SCREENS & STRUCTURES

The simplest type of screen is a self-clinging climber used to enhance a wall that would otherwise be monotonous or unsightly. However, this elementary alliance between plants and architecture can be taken much further. By building a screen, pergola, arbour or arcade, you can provide not only a fine support for climbing plants but also a structure that offers ornamental interest in its own right and helps to increase the appeal of the garden by subdividing the plot into distinct areas.

CAMOUFLAGE

In the garden, everyone has something to hide. It is rare to find a garden that does not contain an ugly stretch of perimeter wall, an all-too functional garage or an unprepossessing shed – not to mention the shortcomings of the house itself. All too often, the back of the house has been left undesigned, as if it were of no importance. Extensions tend to be tacked on without regard for aesthetics.

The obvious solution is to plant the fastest-growing species – for example, Russian vine, *Clematis montana* or virginia creeper. However, all three have a tendency to romp away at great speed and will soon disappear into the heights, leaving the lower stems bare – which will only accentuate the problematic wall surface.

Another solution, though one that requires a little patience, is to grow a mixture of evergreen, deciduous and flowering climbers. These will provide year-round interest and eventually become dense enough to cover any structure. The choice of plants, of course, will depend on the orientation and the soil. If you have a sunny, frost-free wall, you could grow *Ceanothus* × *delilianus* 'Gloire de Versailles'. This evergreen will grow to 7 feet (2m). In the spring it flowers so profusely that the leaves are almost invisible beneath a froth of powder-blue flowers which bees and other insects find irresistible. After flowering, the forward-growing branches can be cut back hard to encourage the shrub to develop up and across the wall.

Certain clematis can be recommended to take over from the *Ceanothus* once it has ceased to flower. 'Lady Betty Balfour', a purple large-bloomed hybrid with golden stamens, flowers from mid-summer through to early autumn. The species *Clematis tangutica*, often sold as *C. orientalis*, has many cultivated forms. They are commonly known as orange-peel clematis on account of their thick rich yellow sepals. (The cultivar 'Orange Peel' is in fact a form of the

LEFT *A garage disappears under an autumn mantle of quick-growing* Parthenocissus tricuspidata. *The pile of logs also helps to disguise the rather stark effect of modern brickwork.*

ABOVE *An oil storage tank, unexpectedly colourful, has been artfully combined with the blue-green leaves and red berries of* Cotoneaster horizontalis *to turn a potential eyesore into a harmonizing composition.*

closely related *C. vernayi*.)

Wall shrubs that have an architectural habit can also be used for camouflage – for example, *Pyracantha coccinea*, notable for its berries, and *Chaenomeles* × *superba*, whose flowers vary from glistening white to deep vermilion. A wall shrub that remains interesting throughout the year is *Cotoneaster horizontalis*. In winter its appeal comes from the herringbone pattern of branches. It is useful in a difficult, dry situation.

Planting for disguise will be doubly effective if you choose plants that integrate into the colour scheme of the rest of the garden. The eye will then see the garden as a continuous composition. Painting the offending wall in a harmonizing or even contrasting hue can also help to improve the aesthetics.

If you need a service area in the garden for tool shed, dustbins and so on, you can sometimes hide it successfully by a climber-clad trellis with loose wall shrubs grown behind. This has the effect of making us feel that there is a whole new area of garden behind the screen.

Hedges also make good screens (see pages 42–47), but for something different try bamboos. Commonest are members of the genus *Arundinaria*. They like a reasonably moist soil, but be warned: both *A. anceps* and *A. japonica* can become invasive if the soil is *too* damp. *Arundinaria japonica* is the tallest of the common bamboos, growing up to 18 feet (6m). *Arundinaria anceps* grows to about 10 feet (3.5m) and has dark green glossy stems and leaves. If the situation calls for something smaller, *A. viridistriata* reaches about 6ft (2m), its deep green leaves boldly striped with yellow bands which are brighter on new growth. Two other attractive species, both of which grow to about 10 feet (3.5m) and have bright green leaves, are *A. spathaceus*, whose canes mature to yellow-green, and *A. nitida*, with purple-flushed canes.

THE DIVIDED GARDEN

The Persians, the Romans and the Mughals are among the ancient peoples who divided their gardens into a series of smaller enclosed spaces. To this day, many of the most famous and best-loved gardens have been designed on the same principle: a series of self-contained gardens that all have a different theme. By this means it is possible to divide a large unwelcoming space into distinct areas, each on a human scale, each offering a different kind of enjoyment, whether exciting or peaceful.

At the same time, a theatrical touch can be introduced, so that over and over again, you can experience surprise – a vital ingredient in garden design. Each space will beckon you on and lead you through the garden. One way to achieve this is to make an *enfilade* of openings, at the end of which is a wall plaque, a waterspout, an urn or a statue. This will not only draw the visitor down the axis to see what lies at the end, but can also create remarkable effects of perspective. The eye is naturally drawn to the focal point, and this increases the feeling of depth – obviously an important factor in a small plot.

It is a nice idea to give each subdivision of the garden a name. This would usually refer to its main theme. You could have a Blue or Red Garden, a Box or Rose Garden. Other choices might be: a Scented Garden, where all the different smells would be trapped by the boundaries, which themselves would consist of scented shrubs and climbers; a Water Garden, with a fountain in the centre, simple or grand, or a rill along the axis; a Pot Garden; or a Sculpture Garden. Each one might be planned to look its best at a certain time of day or a certain time of the year.

The dividing screens may be solid so that they reveal, from the outside, nothing of the space they enclose. The effect as you pass from one style or theme to another will then be one of total surprise. If it's a hedge, you can cut a window into it to increase the communication between the separate areas – just as you can make windows (or *clairvoyées*) in walls or solid gates. Such openings give a taste of things to come, and the art lies in not revealing too much.

The larger the garden, the more scope there is to vary the disposition of the paths and openings. If you create a meandering route that takes unexpected turns, you will entice the visitor onward to see what lies beyond the next obstacle.

The greater the variety between the styles and themes of each subdivision, the more important it is that the dividing walls, screens or hedges provide continuity throughout the garden. This

Openings between one garden compartment and the next can take a number of forms. Both examples on these pages are surrounded by roses which encroach into the opening and soften its hard-edged geometric lines.

RIGHT *The circular window in this lichen-mottled grey wall is precisely placed above a stone bench. Anyone curious about the view beyond could stand on the bench to peep through.*

LEFT *This feature also relies on high-quality masonry. The arch frames a superb urn beautifully planted with begonias and nasturtium 'Alaska'.*

RIGHT *One of the main circulation routes in this garden is bordered by* Camellia *'Donation', which puts on a spectacular show of flowers in early spring before most other plants have begun to flower. For the rest of green hedge against which flowering shrubs and herbaceous perennials can be seen at their best.*

CENTRE *Roses 'Gold Finch' and 'Frances E. Lester' climb over a complex arrangement of timber screens and pergolas, forming continuity between several garden compartments. The succession of openings creates an enticing vista.*

is why sombre yew and undemonstrative box are so often chosen for the basic structure.

Make sure that the screens do not conflict with the style of the garden they enclose. It would not suit a formal water garden to be flanked by an informal flowering hedge or screens of trelliswork laden with a varied collection of climbers: more in keeping would be a tightly clipped yew hedge or a simple trellis fence with classical-style finials on the posts. The flowering hedge is best reserved for a larger shrubbery. Trelliswork adorned with climbers would be particularly appropriate for a patio, or a cottage garden in which questions of time or money have precluded the choice of a hedge or walls.

FENCES AND TRELLISES

Fences, all too often, are treated as merely functional elements, used to define boundaries and defeat prying eyes. Solid fences tend to be smothered in plants or tolerated only until hedges have grown up to take their space. However, openwork fences, serving either to screen areas within the garden or to mark the perimeter, offer a range of more exciting possibilities. Although limited from the privacy point of view, they have all the versatility of trelliswork, providing a framework whose geometric form can be used to complement the natural growth of plants.

An open fence can be assembled from slats arranged horizontally, vertically or diagonally across a simple framework. One of the most familiar types is the picket fence, which has a multitude of decorative forms, achieved by varying the heights of the palings, the spacing between them and the treatment of picket tops and post tops. For example, picket tops may be pointed, spade-shaped, spear-head, angle-cut, or double or triple saw-toothed. Using pickets graduated in height between each pair of posts you can create a curved profile, either convex or concave. Or you can alternate long and short pickets to create either a stepped effect along the top or a two-tier effect, the fence becoming more open above the half-way mark.

Trellis is inexpensive, comes in different weights, is relatively easy to erect and, like open fencing, offers plenty of design variations. The laths can be arranged in squares or lozenges, and can be used in double thickness to add depth and visual solidity. I have seen a trellis patterned with lozenges on a slant, but this was unsettling to the eye: such distracting designs are best avoided. Trellis is the ideal material to make a unifying link in garden design, whether used against a wall or in a freestanding structure. Its colour may be chosen to blend with the overall colour theme of the garden or the paintwork of the house, or, specifically, to complement the flowers for which it acts as a support. If you build your own trellis, instead of relying on pre-fabricated units,

RIGHT *The rose-covered trellis screens that demarcate this sitting area are just the right height to provide privacy without being out of scale with the rest of the garden. The arch pattern and turned finials add a touch of distinction. On the sunnier side are clumps of hebe, while on the shadier side are colourful* Impatiens, *or busy lizzies.*

you can make the spacing wider or narrower to suit different plants.

Painted timber structures usually need repainting every two years or so, depending on the climate, but this will be difficult if they have become overgrown. So, instead of shrubby climbers, you might try growing annual or herbaceous perennial climbers that die down in winter – perhaps sweet peas, the less hardy but vigorous *Cobaea scandens*, or the tender annual morning glory (*Ipomoea tricolor*, preferably 'Heavenly Blue', with sky-blue flowers).

LEFT *Sweet peas and wisteria grow over an arch constructed from narrow panels of trellis held together to form openwork columns and cross-pieces, and painted blue-grey to form a subtle background to the plants.*

BELOW *A picket fence in eye-catching white, with arrow-head pickets, makes an excellent boundary bordering the street. The "high-low" method of construction ensures that the fence is animal-proof at the bottom but open at the top so that foliage and flowers can spill through the gaps. The informal hedge behind the fence is of the modern shrub rose 'Nevada'.*

BELOW *A substantial white-painted trellis wall along a driveway provides a support for boxes planted according to the season. This view, taken in summer, shows petunias, pelargoniums, lobelia and trailing mother-of-thousands echoing the colour of the pink roses trained in hoops along the bottom of the structure. The garden reminds us that window boxes are more versatile than their traditional use on window sills might suggest.*

PERGOLAS AND ARBOURS

Originally designed for warm climates to provide a shaded place to walk or sit, pergolas have deservedly been adopted in cooler regions for their structural interest and the opportunities they give for growing beautiful climbers.

Pergolas can be dramatic but will dominate the garden if they are not positioned correctly. Consider siting one near the house on the warm, sunny side or, in a small garden, along one of the boundaries, using the perimeter wall as a support. A pergola could also be used instead of a hedge as a division between, for example, the flower garden and the vegetable garden.

In accord with its traditional function as a walkway, a pergola should always lead somewhere – if only to a seat, statue or wall fountain. Make the most of its capacity for channelling the view to create a splendid vista. On a clear day, bands of shadow across the path will create an attractive rhythm, swinging round as the sun changes position. On a wet day a pergola will drip for some time after the rain has stopped, but this one practical disadvantage is outweighed by the aesthetic contribution the structure can make.

An arbour – essentially, a modest open structure of metal or wood, often enclosing a seat – offers similar pleasures on a smaller scale. It should be positioned in the sunniest spot in the garden, either as the central feature of one compartment, or as the focal point for the whole design, perhaps at the intersection of crisscrossing paths. Put a roof on, and you have a summer house. Both arbours and summer houses are intended to provide a quiet place in which to sit and contemplate – preferably amid wreaths of fragrance.

Such structures must be solidly built, aesthetically pleasing and an integral part of the garden design. It is a mistake to think of them solely as a prop for plants, because in winter the bare bones of the structure will be revealed in all its

ABOVE *A scramble of honeysuckle, roses and clematis disguises a simple framework made of rustic poles. This kind of structure can be made as an arbour, a pergola or an arcade without difficulty.*

LEFT *An avenue made of tall trellis pyramids sheathed in roses makes an alternative to a pergola. This one is in the rose garden at L'Haÿ-les-Roses near Paris. Two English climbing roses make an alternating succession – 'Mrs F.W. Flight' and 'Paul's Scarlet Climber'. Raised at the beginning of this century, these roses are now largely superseded by other cultivars; however, they are contemporary with the garden itself.*

CENTRE *This tile and stone pergola has a presence of its own right during the winter months, but in summer supports pink roses and clematis.*

splendour – or horror, depending on the materials and method of construction.

An inexpensive framework can be built of wood, using 4×4 inch (10×10cm) timber for both uprights and cross beams, weatherproofed by staining or painting. Ensure that any preservative you use is not toxic to the plants that you plan to grow. In a country garden, at some distance from the house, rustic poles – which retain their bark – might be more appropriate, as they give a more informal look. Alternatively, it is possible to buy metal or wrought-iron frames suitable for building round-topped pergolas (more strictly termed "arcades").

A pergola may also be a more substantial structure with stone, brick or tile columns supporting heavy timber crosspieces. This style was popularized by the architect Sir Edwin Lutyens at the beginning of this century. Mellow brickwork piers look particularly good as a background for red roses. The proportions need care – all too often, the superstructure is too flimsy in relation to the supports. Attention to detail will always pay off: for example, cutting the ends of the timber members to slope outward instead of finishing square will make a more attractive finish. Diagonal cross-braces can be used to good effect, at least on the arches at each end of the structure. Panels of trellis may also be incorporated into the structure, although you should avoid making it too complicated.

Plants for pergolas, arcades, arbours and summer houses must be vigorous enough to cover the structure adequately – nobody likes to see wispy plants struggling limply up a column. However, the plants should not swamp the frame totally, or the result will be a dark, gloomy tunnel. Correct cultivation will encourage good strong growth; and pruning will restrain overgrowth.

The classic combination of honeysuckle, roses and clematis will make a wonderful spectacle on

FAR LEFT *A white-painted architectural arbour, serving as a gateway, makes a strong impact in a recently planted garden. At each corner grows the vigorous crimson rose 'Blaze', which will soon spread across the top.*

LEFT *The climbing rose 'Spartan' reaches the top of this classical column – one of the matching supports for a grand pergola. The ornamental treatment of the timber cross-members accords well with the detailing of the stone capital.*

RIGHT *The fragrant rose 'Sanders' White Rambler' has begun to cover the cross-beams of a wood and brick pergola, meeting a pink rose stationed on the adjacent pillar. Notice the attractive decorative treatment to the ends of the timbers. 'Sanders' White Rambler' is a rose that flowers once in early summer: it should be pruned only to remove faded blooms and dead and diseased wood.*

a pergola or arbour in late spring to summer. Wisteria is also popular. The period of interest can be extended by including other plants. For example, for a pale green background from spring to autumn try the golden form of the beer hop (*Humulus lupulus* 'Aureus'). This is a herbaceous perennial and therefore dies right down in the winter, but during the growing season will reach 20 feet (6m). It is particularly attractive for its pale, papery green flowers.

Also good for autumnal interest are the various fruiting climbers, many of which have vividly coloured autumn leaves. One of the more interesting is *Akebia quinata* which, in a good year, has peculiar sausage-like grey fruit which split open to reveal black seeds. Although somewhat vigorous, it is very hardy and has the advantage of being equally attractive in the late spring when it is covered with purple flowers.

For centuries, vines have been grown over pergolas in Italy. Not only will they bear fruit in warm sunny gardens, but some varieties have spectacular autumnal tints – particularly the hybrid 'Brant' and the Teinturier grape, *Vitis vinifera* 'Purpurea'. Two other grapevine cultivars that are well worth trying are 'Apiifolia', which has deeply divided leaves, and 'Incana', whose leaves are covered with a thick white down.

Laburnum is excellent for creating spectacular flowering tunnels with beautiful yellow tassels. If you want a completely enclosed walkway, you will need to buy bush laburnums ('feathered maidens') and plant them at 4 feet (1.2m) intervals; while for an open-sided tunnel you will need standard trees planted at 6–8 feet (1.8–2.4m) intervals. The strong young shoots should always be tied below the frame, not above, or

they will grow up and break the ties. The laburnum walk will look all the prettier for being underplanted with herbaceous perennials such as the blue *Brunnera macrophylla* or bulbs that flower at the same time – for example, purple *Allium rosenbachianum* or yellow lily-flowered tulips 'West Point' in a sea of blue forget-me-nots.

By practising the ancient art of pleaching trees, you can make an interwoven tunnel of greenery – a kind of living pergola – without the need for an artificial structure. Suitable species that are pliable enough to submit to this kind of torture include lime, plane, hornbeam, yew, box, holly, whitethorn and privet. In the early stages you will need to support the young plants on a frame of wire, but in time the lateral branches will knit together and the framework can then be taken down.

LEFT *A wisteria climbs up a wooden framework overhanging a pool along one boundary wall of the garden. A corrugated plastic roof (hidden from view by the plant) admits sufficient light to grow a few shade-tolerant species. The little fountain and the Japanese stone lantern contribute to an atmosphere of cool and repose.*

RIGHT *A series of iron arches is the simple basis for this dreamy tunnel of white* Wisteria floribunda *'Alba'. An interesting way to distinguish* W. floribunda *from* W. sinensis *is that the stems of the former spiral clockwise, while those of the latter spiral anti-clockwise. On the left there is a hint of yellow* Laburnum × vossii.

BELOW *A simple trellis arbour in a vegetable garden is clothed, on its shady side, with the golden hop, Humulus lupulus 'Aureus'. This is a herbaceous perennial and dies down completely during the winter, revealing the structure that supported it. On the sunny side of the arbour, hidden from view, a grapevine takes advantage of the more sympathetic conditions. The upper part of the structure has a triangular pediment, which gives it a distinctly classical feel.*

CHANGING THE LEVEL

A garden on more than one level is intrinsically a more interesting kind of space. Not the least of its merits is the increased range of planting options made possible by extra surfaces in the vertical plane. The simplest version of the multi-level garden is one that carries the planting up existing walls by means of window boxes and hanging baskets – an excellent strategy where space is limited. More ambitiously, you could create a series of terraces linked by steps; and if the steps are wide enough they could be used as a platform for container plants to provide a versatile display of colour that changes with the seasons.

HANGING GARDENS

For many people, window boxes and hanging baskets may be the only means available of enjoying any kind of garden at all. Despite the limitations of their restricted size, some spectacular effects can be achieved, giving pleasure both from inside and outside the house.

My first window boxes were rather rudimentary, consisting of nothing more than planks crudely joined and painted white to contrast with the black cast iron of my window balustrade. The soil drained not through holes drilled in their bases, in the conventional way, but through the gaps in the sides where the warped planks failed to meet satisfactorily. This meant that, until I had worked out a way to adjust the watering regime, one display was always slightly more spectacular than the other as it stayed moist longer!

There are numerous different types of boxes on the market. Reproduction stone made of cement or fibre glass is attractive, if expensive. Plastic boxes, available at most garden centres, have the merit of being light and are reputed to keep the growing medium at a uniform temperature and more constantly moist.

If the box is to be removed for maintenance, handles will help. Alternatively, you could use an inner box lining, which you could lift out without disturbing the heavier outer box. Out of consideration for neighbours and passers-by, secure your box with brackets, unless it is very stable, and use a tray to catch surplus water.

I have two pairs of boxes that I rotate according to the seasons. As soon as my spring boxes are past their best I can replace them with a new set of boxes full of summer annuals. This requires a little more work, and space to store the boxes not on display, but is well worthwhile. I vary the planting most years as new ideas occur to me. For spring, I have particularly enjoyed a mixture of three sorts of narcissus planted in

tiers: nearest the window, the early-flowering small-flowered cultivars 'Tête-à-Tête', or 'February Gold' with 'Beryl', or 'Jack Snipe'; down the middle, *Narcissus triandrus* 'Thalia' for mid-season flowering; and, on the outside edge, the brilliant 'Professor Einstein', which has large orange-red cups.

For late spring, I like a display of tulips: either the tall, lily-flowered tulips 'White Triumphator' or 'China Pink' rising from a sea of pale blue forget-me-nots, or a single planting of the Central Asian species *Tulipa greigii* with its scarlet flowers and beautifully spotted and striped purple-brown leaves.

The spring boxes need to be prepared in the autumn. Choose plump, healthy bulbs that you have bought from a reliable supplier, as diseased plants will ruin the display. The early flowering bulbs can go into the window box, and the later ones kept outside until needed. It should not be necessary to water the boxes at all until the spring, when the leaves are in full growth. The flowers, once they appear, will last longer if the plants are watered at least once a week. Continue watering the bulbs and giving them a weekly liquid feed until the leaves die down, to ensure that the flowers are fully initiated in the bulbs for the following year.

After flowering, daffodil bulbs should be buried under a good covering of soil in the garden until they are needed for planting again in the autumn: this releases the box for summer planting. Tulips, once the leaves have died down completely, should be lifted and stored on a dry airy shelf until replanting in the autumn: if left in the ground, they tend to divide and lose vigour.

Summer boxes are prepared in the spring. I like the traditional combination of bright red pelargoniums with white alyssum and blue trailing lobelia. I have also grown a mixture of dwarf and standard Swiss Balcony geraniums, all of a strong purple colour to complement the ochre-yellow velvet curtains in my room.

More recently I have grown the half-hardy perennials *Osteospermum ecklonis* 'Whirligig' and *Helichrysum petiolare*. Because the winter was mild, these plants have provided me with a continuous display of green and grey foliage. All I needed to do in the spring was to clip them back and they were ready to put on another display of flowers for the summer.

BELOW *Brightly coloured mimulus cultivars and blue lobelia will grow well in a window box in cool climates. Seed sown under glass in early spring will flower the same year. Again, the box itself is discreetly black.*

LEFT *A winter composition of cyclamen backed by a small evergreen conifer and flanked by two long trailing ivies accentuates the elongated form of this tall narrow window. The window box is painted black so that it disappears in shadow, putting the emphasis on the plants.*

ABOVE *Dark red pelargoniums in an unpainted wooden window box contrast strikingly with the bright yellow walls all around. The purple of the wisteria, when it comes into flower, will also complement the wall colour.*

All these ideas assume that your window sills receive plenty of sunlight. For shadier positions, make the most of spring bulbs. Later in the year, a good choice would be ivies and busy lizzies (*Impatiens*).

Hanging baskets are the ideal solution for growing a wide variety of plants if you only have a very small paved yard. They should only be planted out after the last frosts, as most of the small plants you will want to put into the baskets will be tender.

Although many gardeners line their baskets with polythene, or with compressed-peat basket liners, I prefer a good layer of moss for holding the compost in. The compost itself should be as light as possible to make the basket easier to handle. An all-peat mix is fine if you have plenty of time to water and feed the baskets: it is free-draining and dries out relatively quickly. Potting compost with added peat will provide more nutrients through the growing season and extend the life of the plants.

Ivy-leaved pelargoniums, trailing lobelia, petunias and fuchsias are the plants most commonly used in hanging baskets, but you could also try many of the annual climbers such as *Thunbergia alata* and *Cobaea scandens* and the more delicate perennial climbers, such as *Clematis montana* and *Ampelopsis brevipedunculata*. The piggy-back plant (*Tolmiea menziesii*), small-leaved ivy, helxine and silver-leaved ivy together make good all-year-round baskets of greenery if positioned in a sheltered spot for the winter.

Garden soil is heavy, and may need to be made lighter to prevent strain on hanging baskets or to make window boxes easier to lift. To achieve this, there are various other materials you can incorporate. For example, a mixture of peat, vermiculite and a proprietary compost with a little slow-release fertilizer would make an ideal medium for most plants. The nutrients can be topped up

through the growing season with liquid feed applied when you water. It is best to discard old compost at the end of every year and start the new growing season with a fresh mixture, otherwise the plant growth will not be vigorous enough to give a dense display.

Watering is a most important task. Immediately after planting in boxes and baskets, water thoroughly. If you have bought bedding plants in pots, make sure that the root balls are sufficiently moist before planting by giving the pots a good soak overnight. For window boxes, the only plants I would consider leaving in their pots are pelargoniums, as they flower more freely if their roots are restricted.

While the new plants are getting themselves established, they will need watering only once a week, but as the season advances the frequency will have to be stepped up. At the height of the

LEFT *On an elegant Regency balcony in early spring, the combination of yellow and white makes a display of wallflowers in pots, window boxes and hanging baskets particularly distinguished. It is best to choose a dwarf variety for such restricted conditions: seeds come in both single-colour packets and mixed packets. Wallflowers are biennials and should be sown in early summer and grown on the following season. Before planting them in their flowering position, you should pinch them back so that they bush out.*

summer, water at least once daily, preferably in the morning. Many people wrongly assume that rainwater will supply most of the plants' needs. In fact, because hanging baskets and window boxes are sheltered by the eaves of the house, they receive little rain except for a slight sprinkling that does no more than freshen the leaves.

If the soil dries out completely, it will need to be watered a little at a time every hour or so until full capacity has been reached. If you add a lot of water at once, it will simply run off the surface of the soil and down the gap between the soil and the sides of the box. The best cure for a dried-up hanging basket is to immerse it in a bowl of water until the soil is saturated.

To encourage growth sufficient to completely hide a hanging basket, you need to add liquid feed at half strength once or twice a week.

RIGHT *Swiss balcony geraniums at their peak in mid-summer adorn two dormer windows and a skylight. The secret of their flowering is a well-exposed sunny position, and not too much water and nutrients, as these would encourage excessive growth of leaves.*

FAR RIGHT *A cottage garden door is surrounded by a collection of baskets, boxes and pots which contain a profusion of flowering annuals and tender perennials, including begonias, fuchsias, lobelia, busy lizzies and ivy-leaf pelargonium. The flower colours are beautifully offset by the stark black and white of the paintwork.*

LEFT *The beautiful front of a Venetian canal house is enhanced by thinly growing* Parthenocissus tricuspidata *and, on the balcony, boxes of the single-coloured bright red half-hardy annual* Salvia splendens.

ABOVE *A single pink pelargonium in a well-weathered clay pot supported on an elaborate iron bracket makes a simple and effective statement.*

RIGHT *Small pots on a window sill offer a versatile option, as they can be moved around at will, even when the plants are in flower. Here, a simple display of pelargoniums in three clay pots reflects a harmonizing group below.*

ABOVE *A hanging basket between two windows balances the foliage of wisteria, while window boxes below provide a mass of colour. Pelargoniums link the basket and window boxes: these tender perennials come in* *many shades, including reds, pinks, and white, and some have variegated leaves. They can be grown as pot plants indoors through the winter. The basket also contains fuchsia, and grey leaves of cineraria as an accent amid all that colour.*

Below *Blooms of ivy-leaf pelargoniums complement the colour of a fluted cast-iron vase on a decorative wall bracket.*

Left *Hanging baskets make an intermediary level between window boxes and ground-level tubs and pots. The plants include petunias, geraniums, nasturtiums, Calceolaria and trailing lobelias. Boston ivy clads the wall.*

TERRACES, STEPS AND POTS

Terracing is the only satisfactory way to cultivate a steep slope, and has been practised for centuries. It is one of the dominant features of great formal gardens – sets of three or more broad terraces, each with an intricately designed parterre. Today this is the preserve of the rich. But the kind of terraced garden I would like to see more of is the small plot belonging to a house built on the side of a hill.

The task of moving soil to cut and fill from one level to the next is a laborious one, but satisfying during the early or late winter when there is little else to do in the garden and the ground is not frozen. The smaller the garden, the narrower the terraces will need to be to retain the right proportions. A width of between 2½ feet (75cm) and 6½ feet (2m) would be enough to include borders. In the wider beds you could plant small shrubs and large herbaceous perennials; narrower borders could accommodate small herbaceous and rock plants.

Each terrace needs a retaining wall, and in this can be incorporated many small rock and wall plants (see pages 64–69). When choosing plants, bear in mind that the topmost level will be best drained and therefore driest, while the bottom level will be the most moist.

Low herbaceous plants well-suited to such varied conditions would include hardy geraniums, particularly the species *grandiflorum* and *psilostemon*. The cultivars 'Johnson's Blue' and 'Bressingham Flare' are among the best low herbaceous perennials for reasonably drained sites. They associate particularly well with the creeping silver foliage of *Anthemis cupaniana* and *Stachys olympica*, the dark red *Lobelia cardinalis* and purple heliotrope.

Campanulas also like good drainage and enjoy plenty of sun, while *Alchemilla mollis* and hostas will grow in most situations – although the latter favours slightly more shade or damp.

If you find that one of your plants is not enjoying the position you have chosen, do not be afraid to move it to another terrace, or to take it out of or into the shade.

Steps will be needed to climb the terraces in comfort. They can be built up the centre or to one side but should always be attractive in themselves, without dominating the scene. Build them of bricks, stone or wood, preferably to match the material used in the retaining walls; but, above all, be sure that they are safe.

Steps are always a tempting invitation to explore, especially if they lead to a culminating focal point, however modest. They can be edged informally with small creeping plants or, more ceremoniously, with pots and urns filled with bright flowering plants or more subtle, differently textured foliage plants. If terracing is not practicable, it may be easier to make more of the steps and fill the sloping ground at either side with ground-covering plants such as *Hypericum calycinum*, periwinkle or the rose 'Nozomi'. (For

FAR LEFT Alyssum maritimum *(*Lobularia maritima*) and* Campanula portenschlagiana *have seeded themselves in the interstices of these wide terraced steps. Both plants like dry, well-drained conditions: their roots penetrate deeply between stones.*

LEFT *These stone steps linking two levels are edged with candelabra primulas – a species of waterside and bog plant that thrives in cool, damp situations.*

RIGHT *One way to make the most of a sloping site is to construct a rockery. This requires plenty of labour and a supply of good-quality rock. The art reached its apogee during the Victorian era when both were plentiful. Rock gardens can look spectacular but are difficult to manage, requiring meticulous hand weeding. When the plants are mature they will need replacing if they are not to outgrow their allotted space and thus destroy the rockery's outlines. Here the planting is typically complex, including (from the top) yellow potentilla, blue campanula, pink* Polygonum affine *and a host of ferns.*

more on steps, see page 136.)

The paved surfaces may be used to support pot plants. The best effects depend on a decisive choice of style – whether Italianate and very formal, with simple evergreen shrubs in classical tubs and urns; or a breath of the countryside introduced with a profusion of flowering shrubs, spring bulbs and bright hardy annuals.

Pots come in a great diversity of shapes, sizes and materials. I prefer natural materials such as terracotta, stone or wood. Simple designs are best, but this does not preclude decorative touches. For a formal terraced patio I would choose large terracotta pots with swags around the side or, for larger specimens, Versailles *caisses* painted white. For a country patio, handthrown clay pots in different sizes, or wooden tubs, would be a good choice.

Generally, provided that you have used a good potting compost which contains adequate fertilizer, the prime maintenance requirement of pot plants is watering. This cannot be emphasized enough. Even after rain, the compost will probably still be fairly dry to the touch. In bigger pots less water evaporates because of the greater volume of soil; however, this is balanced by the fact that they contain bigger, thirstier plants.

A good way to evaluate the amount of water required by a plant is to sit the pot in a tray and fill this with water until the water is no longer absorbed by the roots. Very full pots will require two or even three waterings a day in high summer if the plants are going to look their best.

Extra nutrients will also be needed at this time, given as a liquid feed once a week. In addition, permanent plantings need to have the top part of the soil (above the roots) removed and replaced with fresh compost in the early spring. It is also sensible to repot moderately-sized specimens every two or three years: pruning will help maintain their vigour and keep their size within bounds.

LEFT *Uncut stone steps interplanted with thyme, with a bowl of blue-leaved sedum as a focus of interest, have a traditional cottage-garden atmosphere. Both thyme and chamomile release their fragrance as they are walked on – and will come to no harm.*

BELOW *The plants in this varied, multi-level collection of pots are all tender in colder districts, and must be brought indoors at the first signs of frost. They include a marguerite in the decorative clay pot, two standard citrus trees in the white urns and, behind, a geranium. All around are little pots containing cuttings: keeping the containers all together is a good way to simplify the task of watering.*

RIGHT *Stone steps weathered by time climb to a terrace that accommodates harmonizing roses. On the left is a lovely white-flowered* Osmanthus, *well-placed for visitors to enjoy its fragrance.*

LEFT *A steep winding staircase of brick has been used here to make the best use of limited space in a small town garden. The hard edges are softened by the placing of pots and a few trailing plants, such as blue lobelia. Giving emphasis to the foot of the steps is a variegated-leaf geranium. Before ordering bricks for the garden, make sure that they are frostproof.*

UNUSUAL TREATMENTS

A garden is more than the sum of its planting. This section of the book looks at some aspects of vertical gardening that are concerned with design and ornament rather than with horticulture – the use of illusionistic techniques (especially wall treatments) to make a small garden seem bigger, the possibilities offered by running water, and the contribution that can be made by freestanding ornamental features. Such ideas can make a major impact even in a garden intended mainly as a home for a splendid plant collection.

ILLUSIONS

In a small garden a certain degree of illusion is desirable to give the impression of greater space. Often, this is a matter of using vertical surfaces such as screens to make the visitor think that there is more to the view than meets the eye. As we have seen in the chapter on The Divided Garden (pages 74–76), erecting barriers helps to blur the boundaries of the plot so that the observer is unable to distinguish precisely where the garden begins and ends. It is only when a garden is visible to the eye in its totality that we can be certain of its dimensions.

Another way to create a sense of spaciousness is by changing the levels – which has the added benefit of providing more growing space. To make the most of this effect, the divisions between levels should be highlighted in some way. For example, in a terraced garden, tall, fastigiate evergreens positioned on each landing at either side of the steps will effectively draw the eye. To emphasize distance, you could build piers at the foot and head of the steps. The steps could also be made so that they are narrower at the top, increasing the feeling of depth still further.

Such tricks with space and perspective can be performed equally well with plants. For example, on the wall farthest from the house the choice of a small-leaved ivy or a small-flowering climbing rose such as 'Climbing Cécile Brunner', might make the wall appear more distant, whereas a covering of large-leaved plants might appear to bring it closer.

One of the most dramatic methods of extending the garden artificially is to paint a mural on the wall surfaces, choosing a subject that completes the prospect from one of the main viewpoints in the garden. The painting could stand alone, or serve as an all-year backdrop to some feature of the garden, such as a border, small summer house or sculpture.

ABOVE *A wall-painted vista of a seat placed at the focal point of a topiary avenue is complemented by real foliage in front. Painted shadows, and little daisies in the grass path, add to the realism.*

Some subjects are simple enough to be tackled by the amateur: for example, a *trompe l'œil* path meandering toward a fake horizon. However, more complex ideas will need the assistance of a professional artist. An artist's time is costly, so you should make sure before the first meeting that you have a good idea of the effect you want to achieve.

One way to help you decide what kind of mural you would like is to look at some of the many excellent works that have been commissioned for public parks and open spaces. One of my favourites is the mural in the Clinton community garden in New York. The scene depicted is a brick path winding through an illusionistic gap in the wall. In the foreground is a magnolia surrounded by informal beds planted with bright red salvias, white phlox and tobacco plants (*Nicotiana alata*). This mural provided the perfect backcloth on my summer visit, when the planting showed its best, and through the long, cold New York winter would provide a jolly forecast of things to come.

In regions blessed with a longer growing season, the scene should ideally be planned to blend with those plants that take pride of place in the garden for the longest period. It is a good idea to paint spring-flowering subjects in the foreground, so that these will be covered as the months progress by taller-growing herbaceous plants. If you wish you can solve the problem of anachronisms altogether by depicting a subtle evergreen scene, with a statue or architectural feature at the focal point: this would be my own recommendation. For a little humour, you could even plant a real-life climber and train it to grow among the painted evergreens, or up a *trompe l'œil* arbour – defying visitors to distinguish illusion from reality.

Instead of representing natural features such as grass, hedges, trees or flowering plants on a garden or patio wall, you might prefer to create a

LEFT *This more elaborate, architectural mural makes a fine courtyard feature. The niche, fluted urn, columns and masonry joints are all painted. Again the depiction of shadows is very successful. Such illusions must be treated with conviction: here two steps leading up to the painting increase its impact.*

RIGHT *The "window panes" of this door under an arched slatted canopy seem to offer a view of another garden beyond, but in fact they are mirrors reflecting back the house and lawn. The door does not even open, despite the ambivalent invitation of two handles.*

more subtle illusion by painting an architectural element. A false niche or alcove will do much to convey an impression of extra depth. Another trick, using wood instead of paint, is to make an arched trellis panel incorporating an inner arch, with converging lines of trellis connecting the two: if skilfully designed to follow the rules of perspective, this can give the effect of a tunnel receding away from the viewer.

A problem with walls is that they confine the space more emphatically than any other form of barrier. To give the illusion that a wall is pierced, with the garden continuing beyond it, you might like to think about the startling effects that can be achieved with mirrors.

When using mirrors outside there are certain practical considerations. Because the mirror will be exposed to frost and rain, precautions should be taken to protect the silvering at the back by sealing the edges with silicon – the material that is used for sealing gaps where water might seep in bathrooms and kitchens.

Modern mirrors have a harsh, almost brutal reflective quality which may look out of place in the garden. The subtler effect of the mercury-backed mirrors of the 18th century can be captured inexpensively by sandwiching alumin-ium foil between a sheet of plate glass and one of plywood. This gives a much more ambiguous reflection, highly appropriate to a romantic atmosphere.

The illusion of extra space will only be convincing if the edges of the mirror are invis-ible, so obscure them with climbers and other shrubs. If you position an interesting feature, such as a sculpture or water spout, opposite the mirror but some distance away, the reflected image will contribute to an increased sense of space. Another possible treatment is to set a mirror into a lattice of trelliswork: a flowering plant grown along the trellis will seem to have double the number of blooms.

LEFT *A flat* trompe l'œil *trellis behind a border of white and red bedding plants creates an illusory sense of depth, owing to its precise imitation of perspective. It has been coloured to harmonize with the wall behind, and also with the garden furniture.*

WATER FEATURES

Many gardeners contrive canals or pools to evoke purity, repose and refreshment. No less satisfying is the creation of water features in the vertical plane, rather than the horizontal – the pleasure brought to the ear by the sound of falling water, and to the eye by ripples, or flashes of reflected sunlight.

Wall spouts make a dramatic focus without taking up space. A classic arrangement is some kind of a carved mask from which water pours or dribbles into a basin or pool, perhaps with an intermediate level over which it spills before continuing its descent. A more complex treatment would be a series of wall-mounted troughs below the spout, with water spilling from one to the other, perhaps with trailing plants echoing the shape of the tumbling streams. You need a submersible pump for such effects, but avoid cheap ones, which may be short-lived or unreliable. You will also need a power point safely connected to the mains – a matter for expert advice.

Raised tanks, perhaps on pillars of stone, bring water closer to eye level and are safer than pools if there are children around. Where water catches sunlight, it will brilliantly reflect the sky. In the shade, the effect will be dank, mossy and romantic. Keep the water level high, as a half-full tank or pool is a sorry sight. Especially under trees, cleaning is important, as leaves and bird droppings will foul the water.

One of the great pleasures of a water feature is the scope for growing species that need damp or waterlogged conditions. Water lilies (*Nymphaea* species), certain irises (*Iris sibirica* and *I. laevigata*), arum lilies (*Zantedeschia aethiopica*) and marsh marigolds (*Caltha palustris*) all thrive in water, and around the edges you can plant some of the richly-textured species that enjoy a damp atmosphere, such as ferns, hostas and astilbes.

FAR LEFT *Camouflaged chameleon-style by its patination, this romantic gargoyle marks a stage on a tiny stream's descent between two levels of a rockery. The sound of running water contributes to the evocative effect no less than the moss and algae.*

CENTRE *This is a possible solution for those who want the sparkle of water without the expense or upheaval of hydraulics. The "streams" are rods of twisted glass which catch the light.*

LEFT *A severe-looking lion's head pours forth its stream from the top of a pyramid of moss. Such details are always a delight to discover in shady, hidden places.*

VERTICAL DETAILS

Freestanding ornamental features are a desirable ingredient in any garden: without such incidental details the garden design would be incomplete. Obvious examples are statues, urns and sundials, but you can create similar sculptural interest in many other, less expensive ways, as the examples on these pages show. Freestanding features of this kind help to establish the mood and style of your garden. They can be used as boundary markers, to indicate distinct areas within the plot, or simply as focal points that provide all-year interest.

Many plant containers have character enough to fill this role – even conventional clay and terracotta pots and wooden tubs. These, of

ABOVE *Tulips in twin baskets mounted on a post create a bright splash of colour in the sunlight. This might make a welcoming feature in a front garden, near the house.*

LEFT *The vivid green leaves of wisteria cling around a statue of Ceres whose sickle almost suggests that she is about to free herself from the unwanted embrace. Statues of this quality are extremely expensive, but you can buy convincing imitations in reconstituted stone.*

course, work as foils to the plants that they contain, but there are other containers that have an ornamental value in themselves – for example, chimney pots of various heights, great glazed oil jars, or sinks or stone troughs. Such features, with complementary plants, all earn their place in a small paved garden where space is at a premium.

Sculptures and statues are probably the most difficult ornamental features to use successfully. They need to be well-produced in high-quality materials and pleasingly-proportioned to warrant the attention that will inevitably be focused on them. A frumpy, obviously synthetic shepherdess will contribute nothing to the garden's atmosphere.

FAR LEFT *The tall, thin forms of a statue and cactus complement each other alongside a rugged stone wall, making a more interesting feature than either would on its own. Such pairings of the animate and the inanimate are always fascinating.*

LEFT *This unusual freestanding composition incorporates an inverted dustbin lid. The compact juniper and beard-like mat of lacy-petalled border pinks are nicely in balance with each other, between yellow sedum and a bonsaied lilac.*

PLANT DIRECTORY

This last major section of the book is a personal selection of plants suitable for vertical gardening – whether for sunny or shady walls (pages 116–23), for hanging baskets, window boxes or pots (pages 124–7), for rapid growth over pergolas and other structures (pages 128–31) or as hedges (pages 132–35). In each category, the plants illustrated on a double-page are described in detail on the following two pages. The numbers after each entry cross-refer to the illustrations.

PLANTS FOR SHADY WALLS

1 *Garrya elliptica*
2 *Chaenomeles speciosa* (ornamental quince)
3 *Forsythia suspensa*
4 *Kerria japonica*
5 *Lonicera × americana* (honeysuckle)
6 *Hydrangea petiolaris*
7 *Rosa* 'Madame Alfred Carrière'
8 *Clematis* 'Nelly Moser'
9 *Clematis* 'Lasurstern'
10 *Rosa* 'New Dawn'

SPRING

SUMME

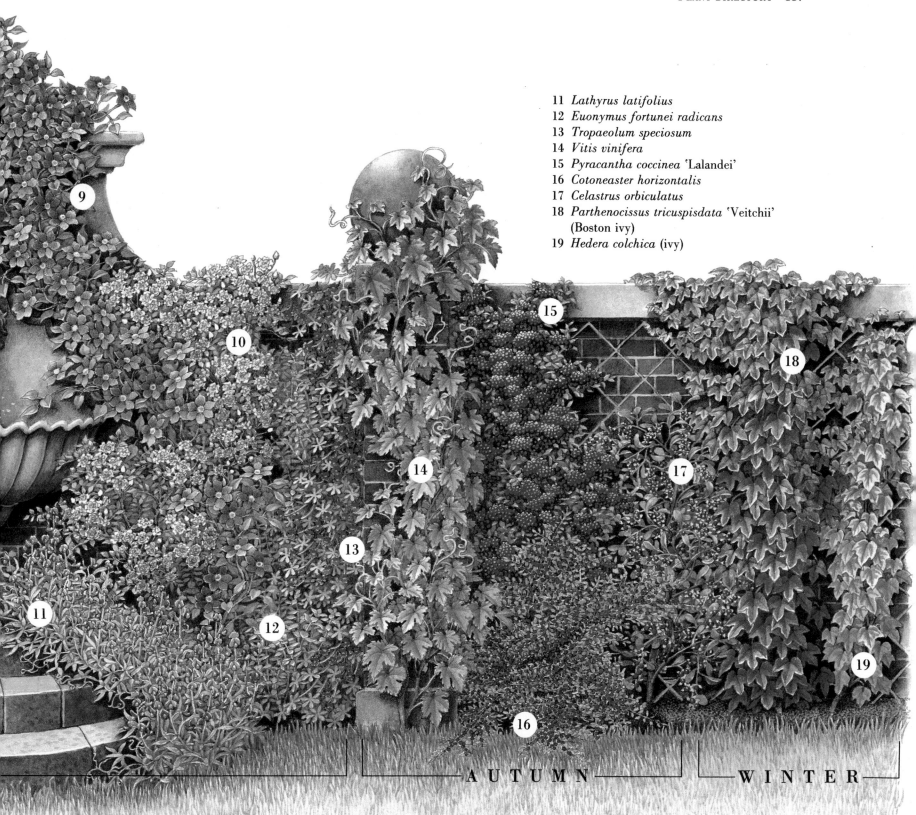

11 *Lathyrus latifolius*
12 *Euonymus fortunei radicans*
13 *Tropaeolum speciosum*
14 *Vitis vinifera*
15 *Pyracantha coccinea* 'Lalandei'
16 *Cotoneaster horizontalis*
17 *Celastrus orbiculatus*
18 *Parthenocissus tricuspisdata* 'Veitchii'
   (Boston ivy)
19 *Hedera colchica* (ivy)

AUTUMN   WINTER

PLANTS FOR SHADY WALLS

These vigorous plants will tolerate the least hospitable sites, including those that receive light and water only in small quantities. Many are suitable for covering eyesores or for growing over a pergola or arbour. In more favourable situations, the plants are likely to become rampant and cause a nuisance unless rigorously controlled.

Celastrus orbiculatus (17)
Oriental bittersweet

A vigorous climber reaching 40 feet (12m) if scrambling up a tree, or 20 feet (6m) on a shady wall. It climbs by twining its young stems around a support; each stem has fierce spines either side of the first buds. The rounded leaves turn golden yellow in autumn, and the yellow fruits split open to reveal bright red seeds which persist through the winter long after the leaves have fallen. Be sure to buy the hermaphrodite strain for successful fruiting.

Chaenomeles speciosa (2)
Japonica/Ornamental quince

The ornamental quince grows well against a wall, flowering early in spring, often producing plump, yellow fruits in the autumn. Pruning and training will ensure healthy upward growth, otherwise branches tend to grow forward from the base. The species flowers are a rich vermilion but there are many cultivars including the white 'Nivalis', the pink, semi-double 'Phylis Moore' and the crimson 'Cardinalis'. Grow in light shade for best fruiting.

Clematis 'Lasurstern' (9)

One of the most beautiful of the blue clematis. The flowers are 6–7 inches (15–18cm) wide and cover the whole plant in early summer, with a second, lesser flush of slightly smaller flowers in early autumn. Each flower has seven or eight broadly overlapping, pointed sepals; the stamens are a contrasting creamy-white. 'Lasurstern' is vigorous, reaching 10 feet (3m). Prune lightly in early spring: cut out dead vines and shorten most of the other stems to the first pair of plump buds. In a shady position cut a small number of vines right down to a foot (30cm) to ensure plenty of renewal.

Clematis 'Nelly Moser' (8)

Another vigorous clematis growing to 11 feet (3.5m) with large flat flowers, 6½ inches (17cm) wide, of eight pale mauvy pink sepals, each with a central purple bar which bleaches in the sun. Prune as for 'Lasurstern' (above); flowering can be delayed by pruning hard in early spring, making a single, slightly bigger, early autumn crop of blooms instead of the usual two crops.

Cotoneaster horizontalis (16)

A shrub for inhospitable, dry and shady spots. Stiff branches in a herringbone arrangement will grow close to the wall, reaching 3–4 feet (90–120cm). Clothed with pretty pink flowers and round, dark, glossy-green leaves in spring. In the autumn it is covered with red berries that can last through the winter. Prune only to cut out old branches.

Euonymus fortunei radicans (12)

A very hardy plant, which clings by means of short aerial roots and reaches 12 feet (3.5m) or more depending on the form. Like ivy, it has a juvenile phase in which it produces small, oval, loosely-toothed leaves. Once it stops climbing, it bears larger leaves as well as flowers and fruit. Good cultivars include 'Silver Gem', with white variegated leaves, 'Coloratus' with reddish-purple leaves during the winter, and 'Vegetus', an adult form that freely bears deep orange berries in autumn.

Forsythia suspensa (3)

Without the bright yellow flowers of forsythia, bringing an early splash of sunshine, spring would be incomplete. It grows to 25 feet (7.5m) and should be pruned immediately after flowering to encourage new growth, which bears the following season's blooms.

Garrya elliptica (1)

A Californian evergreen shrub, which likes a sheltered, shady position but is not very hardy, particularly in the early years. Grows to 20 feet (6m) in mild areas. The male form bears grey, tassel-like catkins 3–6 inches (7–15cm) long. The leaves are oval, dark grey-green above and grey underneath. Prune only to restrict long shoots that may impinge on the flower beds, as it can grow quite wide in maturity. Choose your site well; this plant does not like being moved.

Hedera colchica (19)

This splendid ivy has the largest leaves of the genus – 6–8 inches (15–20cm) long and 4–5 inches (10–12cm) wide, unlobed with the edges rolling over. If crushed, the leathery, light green leaves give off a spicy smell. Grows to over 12 feet (4m) on a wall or pergola. 'Dentata Variegata' has irregularly margined, creamy-yellow leaves; en masse, they make a stunning evergreen background for autumn berrying climbers and wall shrubs.

Hydrangea petiolaris (6)

Also classified as *H. anomala petiolaris*. Slow to establish but will grow to great heights, reaching 50 feet (15m), clinging by small aerial roots. The inflorescences are 6–10 inches (15–25cm) wide in flat clusters of white sterile flowers surrounding small, dirty-white, fertile flowers. They open in early summer and cover the plant. The peeling, rust-coloured bark is appealing in winter. Prune only to restrict exuberance or forward-reaching branches and to guide the plant in the right direction.

Kerria japonica (4)

The double form ('Pleniflora') of this rather stiff, upright shrub was introduced from China in 1804; the more attractive, less commonly grown, wild, single form was not found until 1834. The plant is hardy and grows equally well in sun and shade, reaching 5–7 feet (1.5–2m). It prefers soil that is not too dry. The flowers are deep golden-yellow, many-petalled in the double form 'Pleniflora'. The prolific suckers and the green stems should be cut down soon after flowering to reduce bulk and give space for the following season's flowering stems.

Lathyrus latifolius (11)
Everlasting pea

A perennial climber which grows to about $6\frac{1}{2}$ feet (2m) every year with narrow, grey-green leaves and angular, tangled stems of a similar colour. The flowers grow in dense racemes through most of the summer in varying tones of purple. Tolerates most soils and will give a good show in most positions. The unattractive seed pods can be cut out, though this is not essential. Cultivars include the white forms, 'Albus' and 'White Pearl', the dark purple 'Pink Beauty' and the pink 'Splendens'.

Lonicera × americana (5)

A hybrid often confused with the Early and Late Dutch forms of the common honeysuckle or with one of its parents, L. caprifolium. Attractive and vigorous, reaching 33 feet (10m) in the right conditions, with yellow, flushed, reddish-purple, highly scented flowers in early summer. Prune lightly to remove weak or dead growth, cutting a few stems down to the ground to ensure renewal of growth at the base of the plant, which otherwise tends to become thin and leggy.

Parthenocissus tricuspisdata 'Veitchii' (18)
Boston ivy

This excellent self-clinging climber will grow well almost anywhere. Being very vigorous, it needs lots of space. You may need to restrict the roots and prune severely in summer to prevent it from filling gutters and covering windows. The leaves, broadly lobed with toothed edges, turn bright crimson in the autumn before dropping for the winter. The dark blue berries are rarely seen in cold climates.

Pyracantha coccinea 'Lalandei' (15)

A stiff shrub (evergreen in all but the coldest climates) that can be architecturally trained against a wall. Up to 16 feet (5m) tall with small, shiny, dark green leaves. Covered with small white flowers in early summer and orange berries in autumn and into the winter. Reduce the flowering shoots immediately after blooming and train at the same time. Avoid planting against structures that need regular painting, as it becomes difficult to pull away from the wall.

Rosa 'Madame Alfred Carrière' (7)

This rose was introduced by a French breeder in 1879 and has never lost any of its popularity or vigour. Although of mainly upright habit, it will grow along a wall, reaching 20 feet (6m) with careful pruning and training. The young shoots are bright green, the foliage abundant and the stems have few thorns. The large double flowers start blooming in early summer, peak in mid-summer and bloom again, less profusely, in late summer or early autumn. The sweetly scented buds are pale pink, becoming whiter as they open.

Rosa 'New Dawn' (10)

A healthy, hardy rose, resistant to most diseases, which has given rise to many good perpetual-flowering climbers since its introduction in 1930. Its vigorous lateral habit makes it suitable for shady walls, pergolas and fences. Growth can exceed 15 feet (4.5m) on a wall; prune and train to keep within bounds. The leaves are a shiny light green. The medium-sized flowers are apple-blossom pink with a deeper pink centre, profuse in early summer but continuing to spread their fresh fragrance throughout the season.

Tropaeolum speciosum (13)
Scotch flame flower

A hardy perennial climber with delightful dark crimson flowers from mid-summer to early autumn. Likes the cool conditions found in the shade of a wall or under evergreen hedges and free-standing shrubs. It has deep-rooted, creeping rhizomes from which long strands with pale green, lobed leaves emerge in the spring, spreading up to 10 feet (3m). It needs no pruning.

Vitis vinifera (14)
Grape vine

The grape vine grows vigorously, reaching 12 feet (3.5m) in one season; left to its own devices, it will achieve 25 feet (8m) in height. Cut back the long shoots in summer and prune again just above a pair of plump buds in late winter. It will fruit successfully in a shady position. Attractive variants include the Teinturier grape (V. vinifera 'Purpurea') whose young white leaves turn pale claret-red and slowly darken through the season to dark purple in the autumn.

PLANTS FOR SUNNY WALLS

1 Apple cultivars
2 Peach cultivars
3 *Clematis armandii*
4 *Wisteria floribunda*
5 Cherry cultivars

6 *Actinidia kolomikta*
7 *Clematis* 'Ernest Markham'
8 *Rosa* 'Royal Gold'
9 *Ipomea tricolor* (morning glory)
10 *Magnolia grandiflora*

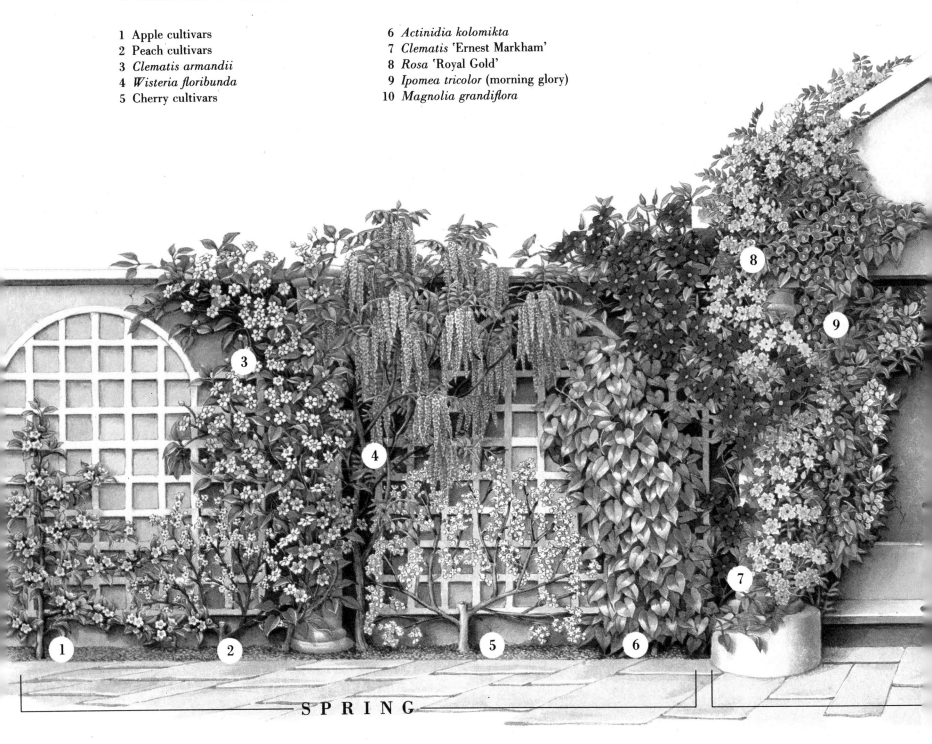

SPRING

11 *Cobaea scandens*
12 *Rosa* 'Zéphirine Drouhin'
13 *Abelia* × *grandiflora*
14 *Solanum crispum* 'Glasnevin'
15 Pear cultivars

16 *Campsis radicans* (trumpet vine)
17 *Ampelopsis brevipedunculata*
18 Fig 'Brown Turkey'
19 *Chimonanthus praecox* (winter sweet)

UMMER · AUTUMN · WINTER

PLANTS FOR SUNNY WALLS

These are mostly tender or marginally tender plants that need summer sun to ensure that the new season's wood ripens adequately to survive the winter. They also benefit from the extra warmth stored in winter by a sunny wall. Once established, all need the relatively dry conditions to be found at the base of any wall. Many of these plants are beautiful, and rewarding to grow, but need more attention than usual.

Abelia × grandiflora (13)

A graceful evergreen shrub growing to 6 feet (1.8m) in a sheltered, warm position. As a hybrid, it is hardier than either parent, but not reliably so in colder districts. Its arching stems have shiny dark leaves. The flowers, which appear in late summer, just as others are beginning to fade, are funnel-shaped, pinky-white and very slightly scented. Prune lightly in autumn when flowering is over. Related to the honeysuckle, this plant likes moist, loamy soil that will not dry out in summer.

Actinidia kolomikta (6)

A hardy climber, related to the Chinese gooseberry, grown for its strikingly variegated green, white and pink leaves which are heart-shaped, up to 6 inches (15cm) long. The plant reaches 10 feet (3m) and needs pruning in winter to build up a strong framework. Cats are strangely attracted to it and may destroy young plants.

Ampelopsis brevipedunculata (17)

This deciduous climber needs some help and guidance in the first year or two, and supports must be provided for its tendrils to cling to. The lobed leaves are dark green above, paler and hairy below. The great attraction is the beautiful fruit which starts off white, turns a delicate china-blue and finally deep purple at the end of a hot summer. It does best on a sunny wall, reaching 8 feet (2.5m). Root restriction encourages fruiting and hardening of the wood, which enables the plant to survive the winter.

Apple cultivars (1)

Apples benefit greatly from being grown against a warm sunny wall. Cordons and espaliers are traditional methods of training: their growth is easily restrained if they are grafted on certified dwarfing rootstock (see page 61). 'Cox's Orange Pippin' is one of the best known apples but is prone to mildew and canker and does not always succeed. In addition to the varieties mentioned on page 61, try the early fruiting 'Tydeman's Early', the mid-season 'Gravenstein' or the late 'James Grieve'. All cultivars require a pollinator and should be pruned in winter and summer. Apples will grow in any soil so long as a reasonable quantity of nutrients and water are available.

Cherry cultivars (5)

If you have only space for one tree, plant the completely self-fertile 'Morello', which is one of the finist acid cherries with large dark red to black fruit ripening in mid-summer, or 'Montmorency', which has huge fruit that can be eaten fresh or cooked. Sweet cherries, even on the dwarfing rootstock 'Colt', tend to make larger trees and most need a pollinator. The cultivars 'Early Rivers' and 'Napoleon' can be recommended, although they are not suitable pollinators. Cherries should be grown as fans planted 12–16 feet apart and lightly pruned in early spring.

Campsis radicans (16)
Trumpet vine

This wonderful exotic, self-clinging climber is hardy on a sunny wall. It is deciduous and likes most soils but needs moisture throughout the summer. The main stems cling to the wall with small roots and will reach 35 feet (10.5m). The leaves are composed of small leaflets with coarsely toothed edges. The bright, trumpet shaped flowers are produced in clusters in late summer on the current season's growth. Prune in early spring after the worst frosts. The suckers can be used for propagation.

Chimonanthus praecox (19)
Winter sweet

This fine shrub does well on a warm wall, flowering in the coldest months of the winter. It is deciduous, growing to 8 feet (2.5m) with deep green, narrow leaves that provide a good background for clematis to grow through during the spring and summer. The delicate, fragrant, palest cream flowers have a maroon to purple centre and bloom on the bare twigs. Prune immediately after flowering to remove weak shoots and shape the shrub.

Clematis armandii (3)

This evergreen clematis needs a warm, sheltered position to thrive as it is not fully hardy, but in the right place it will reach about 15 feet (4.5m). Its leaves are composed of narrow, leathery, dark green leaflets with a rich veining pattern. The small, slightly scented flowers have creamy-white stamens and bloom on the previous year's growth, any time during the spring depending on the weather. Prune immediately after flowering, carefully training and thinning the shoots to avoid the build-up of a tangled mass.

Clematis 'Ernest Markham' (7)

One of the best of the large-flowered red clematis, named after William Robinson's head gardener. Vigorous, reaching over 8 feet (2.5m) in a sunny position. The large magenta flowers have six broad, thick sepals 5 inches (13cm) across. Prune lightly in early spring; flowers are borne first in early summer on the previous year's growth and again, more spectacularly, in summer on the new vines.

Cobaea scandens (11)
Cup and saucer plant

This interesting tender perennial is often treated as an annual, as it is easy to raise from seed if sown in warmth. Given support for the tendrils to cling to, it will reach 15 feet (4.5m) in one season – useful for filling a gap on a pergola. The leaves are pinnate with oval leaflets. The bell-shaped flowers are a dirty pale green on opening, surrounded by the green calyx, which opens out around the flower like a saucer; later, the flowers turn dark purple with creamy stamens.

Fig 'Brown Turkey' (18)

Ficus carica, the common fig, is a most ornamental large shrub. Slightly tender, it needs the protection of a warm, sunny wall and, in some colder areas, further winter protection is needed for successful fruiting (see page 63). Figs are particularly vigorous: long shoot growth, which is often produced at the expense of fruit, should be inhibited by pruning the branches in spring, or by restricting root growth (see page 63). The large lobed leaves can be 8 inches (20cm) in span, and may need thinning in summer to allow light to reach the ripening fruit. 'Brown Turkey' can be grown in a container in the coldest climates.

Ipomea tricolor (9)
Morning glory

As its common name indicates, this subtropical climber is best in the morning when the trumpet-shaped flowers (similar to those of bindweed) open wide; they are closed again by noon, so for maximum pleasure plant in a sunny position near a window overlooked by the breakfast table. On a good day the whole plant can be covered with flowers. In colder climates grow as an annual: sow the seed in the warmth in late spring, in tall pots so that they can be transplanted with minimum root disturbance. They will grow to 6 feet (2m) in one season. The leaves are heart-shaped. The most beautiful cultivar is the clear, slightly metallic 'Heavenly Blue'.

Magnolia grandiflora (10)

A magnificent wall shrub if planted in a warm, sunny position, with the added virtue of being tolerant of atmospheric pollution. The large oval leaves are shiny, dark green above and covered with fine, rust-coloured hairs beneath. The great creamy-white flowers can be up to 5 inches (13cm) long, the petals clasped, chalice-like, and wonderfully fragrant. The main stems should be carefully tied to the wall to stop the shrub from breaking in the wind. Prune lightly to contain growth in summer.

Peach cultivars (2)

The old cultivar 'Peregrine' is one of the best available for temperate climates. Peaches should be grown as fans planted on rootstock 'St Julien A'. They require good drainage, and soil that is not too alkaline. Prune in early spring and summer for successful fruiting. Spray with Bordeaux mixture in early spring to minimize leaf curl.

Pear cultivars (15)

Pears always do best in a protected, sunny position, and have much the same cultural requirements as apples, growing in well-drained, but reasonably moisture-retentive soil. Espaliers and cordons grown on dwarfing rootstocks Quince A should be planted 16–23 feet (5–7m) apart; on Quince C 13–16 feet (4–5m) apart. Plant two different cultivars to ensure pollination. Two of the best are 'Williams Bon Chrétien' ('Bartlett'), which ripens in early autumn, and should be eaten at once as it does not store well, and 'Doyenné du Comice' the queen of pears, a late variety that keeps perfectly and has an unctuous texture.

Rosa 'Zéphirine Drouhin' (12)

This rose has many qualities. It is very sweetly scented. It has bright cerise, double flowers which, although small, are borne in great clusters. It flowers with abundance in early summer and continues throughout the season if regularly deadheaded. Being thornless, it is ideal for use on a patio, round a door or by heavily frequented paths. It will reach 10 feet (3m) and can be used with success as a hedge as it does not mind hard pruning. Its only fault is susceptibility to blackspot and mildew, which can be minimized if the plant is grown in an airy place or on a warm, sunlit wall.

Rosa 'Royal Gold' (8)

Bred in the USA and introduced in 1957, this climber of moderate vigour reaches about 10 feet (3m) on a sunny wall. The leaves are a glossy dark green. The golden yellow, double flowers are scented and recurrent from early summer onward but never in great quantity. Deadhead regularly to encourage maximum flowering. Prune only to remove dead and diseased stems.

Solanum crispum 'Glasnevin' (14)

Related to the potato and tomato, this semi-evergreen climber is vigorous in a warm, sheltered position. It prefers well-drained, alkaline soil and grows to 15 feet (4.5m). The flowers are purple-blue with yellow anthers; they begin to open in mid-summer and continue until early autumn, followed by cream-coloured berries which contain many seeds. Gloves should be worn to prune the vines in early spring after the frosts, as the plant has been known to cause a rash.

Wisteria floribunda (4)

The Japanese wisteria only achieves half the height of W. sinensis – reaching 30 feet (9m) or so – but is probably hardier. The two plants are also distinguished by the direction in which the stems twine – W. floribunda spirals clockwise, W. sinensis anti-clockwise. The bluey-mauve flower racemes are shorter, extending to 10 inches (25cm), but equally fragrant. Cultivars include white 'Alba' and pink 'Rosea'. The long shoots need careful guiding so that they do not form a mat of twined wood. They should also be shortened in the summer and again in winter to encourage flowering.

PLANTS FOR CRACKS AND CRANNIES

1 *Asplenium trichomanes*
2 *Arabis albida*
3 *Cheiranthus cheiri* (wallflower)
4 *Erinus alpinus* (foxglove)
5 *Aubrieta deltoidea*
6 *Iberis sempervirens*

7 *Corydalis lutea*
8 *Anthemis cupaniana*
9 *Helianthemum nummularium*
10 *Saxifraga longifolia*
11 *Erigeron karvinskianus*

WINTER   SPRING

PLANTS FOR CONTAINERS

12 *Crocus chrysanthus* cultivars
13 *Viola × wittrockiana*
14 *Iris histroides* (pansy)
15 *Hedera helix* cultivars (ivy)
16 *Muscari armeniacum* (grape hyacinth)
17 *Narcissus* (daffodils)
18 *Primula* (primroses and polyanthus)
19 *Vinca major*

20 *Fuchsia* cultivars
21 *Lobelia erinus*
22 *Tropaeolum majus* (nasturtium)
23 *Petunia × hybrida*
24 *Begonia semperflorens*
25 *Pelargonium*
26 *Lotus berthelotti*
27 *Nicotiana affinis* (tobacco plant)

SUMMER — AUTUMN

CRACKS AND CRANNIES

There is a great variety of alpine and rockery plants available for vertical gardening. Many of these come from alkaline regions, and therefore benefit from the presence of crumbling mortar in the cracks of brick or stone walls.

Anthemis cupaniana (8)

Forms neat cushions of feathery, grey leaves 6 inches (15cm) high with large daisy-like flowers from summer to autumn. Likes well-drained soil and plenty of sun. Propagate from cuttings in autumn (advisable in cold areas) or by division in spring. The variety 'C.E. Buxton' has lemon-yellow flowers.

Arabis albida (2)

Forms loose mats of grey-green oblong leaves with bright, white, slightly fragrant flowers of four petals carried in lax racemes 8 inches (20cm) tall in spring. Plant on a sunny wall or in a crevice. Deadhead after blooming. Propagate from seed or, for the best forms such as the double 'Flore-Pleno', the pink 'Rosabelle' or the green-and-yellow leaved 'Variegata', from cuttings.

Asplenium trichomanes (1)
Maidenhair spleenwort

A hardy fern with pinnate fronds 2–8 inches (5–20cm) high on dark reddy-brown stems. Likes a well-drained mixture of grit and leaf-mould or peat. Often found wild on shady, dry walls. Withstands drought remarkably well. Divide in spring.

Aubrieta deltoidea (5)

At best 4 inches (10cm) tall, but can spread up to 2 feet (60cm). Thrives in dry or well-drained alkaline soils or in perished mortar in crevices. The four-petalled flowers vary in colour from purple to shades of red and mauve. Clip all over after flowering to contain straggly growth.

Cheiranthus cheiri (3)
Wallflower

A fragrant plant, 12 inches (30cm) tall when grown on a wall, often more in open beds. Cultivars have flowers ranging from pale yellow to coppery red from mid-spring to early summer. They like well-drained soil, preferably alkaline. Treat as biennials; sow seed in the open in early summer and plant out in autumn. Once established in a wall, wallflowers spread readily.

Corydalis lutea (7)

A densely tufted, hardy plant with brittle, succulent stems. Succeeds in walls thanks to fibrous roots which follow cracks. Grey-green, fern-like leaves. Golden-yellow flowers in racemes from spring to autumn. Spreads readily by seed once established, and small plants can be tucked into wall crevices.

Erigeron karvinskianus (11)
Fleabane

A herbaceous perennial (formerly called *E. mucronatus*) with tiny daisy-like flowers from late spring to early autumn. Grows in tufted mats of small oval leaves with white flowers, ageing pink, with a yellowy disc. Can become invasive, self-seeding with abandon. May be cut back in a cold winter but will grow again from the crown if planted in a sunny position.

Erinus alpinus (4)
Fairy foxglove

A delightful perennial less than 6 inches (15cm) tall, often less. Racemes of small pink to purple flowers rise above tufted rosettes of small, toothed, oval leaves. Will grow in sun but likes cooler conditions and appreciates shade in warmer climates. Self-seeds easily. 'Albus' is pure white, 'Carmineus' carmine.

Helianthemum nummularium (9)
Rock rose

Short-lived, but adds a splash of brightness to a wall. Orange, yellow, white, red or pink flowers open afresh each morning and shed petals during the day. Well-drained soil, full sun. Clip to retain shape after flowering in mid-summer. Not completely hardy: take cuttings in summer in case some are lost.

Iberis sempervirens (6)

Forms a low, compact cushion of dark evergreen leaves smothered in pure white flowers in spring. The plant will spread to 2 feet (60cm) but is easily contained. 'Little Gem' is a smaller and more erect pink cultivar. Grow in well-drained, slightly alkaline soil.

Saxifraga longifolia (10)

This rock plant, one of a huge genus suitable for growing in walls, has solitary rosettes of strap-shaped leaves; these build up to 1 foot (30cm) across until the plant flowers and then dies. The white flowers are carried in tall, arching sprays which can reach 2 feet (60cm). This plant does not like either full sun or too much shade. Likes well-drained soil with some grit.

CONTAINERS

The plants here – bulbs, annuals (hardy and half-hardy) and tender perennials – are all suitable for containers, whether for hanging baskets or window boxes or to grow on different levels of a terrace or patio. Those that are tender can easily be brought indoors for protection over the winter.

Begonia semperflorens (24)

A half-hardy perennial which makes a pleasant carpet of shining, roundish leaves and numerous small flowers throughout the summer, standing 6–12 inches (15–30cm) high. The species has white flowers and pale green leaves, but hybrids have pink to red flowers with leaves of dark green to bronze. Sow the minute seed with sand in late winter in warmth. Plant out in late spring after the frosts.

Crocus chrysanthus cultivars (12)

In its native Greece, this crocus has yellow petals feathered with purple on the outside. Cultivars range in colour from white ('Snowbunting'), creamy yellow ('Cream Beauty') and golden yellow with a bronze exterior ('Zwanenburg Bronze') to soft blue ('Blue Pearl') or violet-blue with a purple exterior ('Blue Peter'). Grow in well-drained, gritty compost in pots. Plant generously in autumn for a mass of blooms in spring.

Fuchsia cultivars (20)

Most of the hundreds of fuchsia cultivars have spectacular flowers of four petal-like sepals which curl back to reveal the corona (often in a brightly contrasting colour) and long, delicate stamens; some are single, others double. Good cultivars for growing as bushes in pots include 'Princess Dollar' (cerise and violet) and 'Trace' (crimson and white). For hanging baskets try 'Cascade' (white and crimson) or 'Citation' (pink and white). Protect in winter as they are not fully hardy. Cut back and repot as soon as the danger of frost is past.

Hedera helix cultivars (15)
Ivy

For pots choose the self-branching, small-leaved forms such as 'Triton' and 'Chicago' (with deeply cut lobes), or the unlobed 'Luzii' and 'Big Deal'; the leaves of the latter are puckered. Variegated forms include the white-edged 'Anne Marie', grey-and-white margined 'Glacier' and golden-centred 'Peter'. All are hardy and drought-resistant.

Iris histrioides 'Major' (14)

One of the beautiful little irises that flower in late winter, suitable for growing in pots where they can be admired at close quarters. Very hardy, showing deep blue flowers with white and gold markings through the snow. Likes sunshine and requires the good drainage of a light, preferably limy, soil. Other small irises include the many cultivars of the scented blue *Iris reticulata* and the yellow *Iris danfordiae*.

Lobelia erinus (21)

A useful half-hardy annual for window boxes or hanging baskets. Trailing or compact forms can be used together for bold impact, or singly for a more subtle effect. Colours vary from pale blue with white eyes to dark blue, crimson or violet with dark eyes, to totally white. Plant out in early summer.

Lotus berthelotii (26)
Dove's beak

A native of the pine forests of Tenerife, but thought to be extinct in its natural habitat. Its graceful, grey, hairy, hanging foliage reaches 2 feet (60cm) and is patterned with vermilion flowers that stand out well against the leaves. Grow in well-drained compost in a sunny, warm position. Not hardy; protect from frost.

Muscari armeniacum (16)
Grape hyacinth

A good bulbous species to complement daffodils. Likes well-drained, gritty soil and sun. Blue racemes of round, bell-shaped flowers rise above narrow fleshy leaves. Plant in autumn and propagate by separating bulblets at the same time.

Narcissus species and cultivars (17)
Daffodils

Dwarf species are best for pots: *Narcissus cyclamineus* has swept-back petals, and the early cultivars 'February Gold' and 'Tête-à-Tête' often have two nodding flower heads; the white *N. triandrus* 'Thalia' flowers a little later. Larger cultivars give height to the display: try the white 'Mount Hood', the pink cupped 'Passionale' and the orange cupped 'Professor Einstein'. For a good show, plant a generous number of firm bulbs in tiers, in autumn, in a well-drained, gritty, peat-based compost. Start watering when they begin to flower; continue until the leaves die down. Add soluble nutrient to the water once a week to build up the bulbs for next season.

Nicotiana affinis (27)
Tobacco plant

Sweetly scented when the flowers open in the evening, from mid-summer until the first frosts. A bushy plant, up to 3 feet (90cm) tall with large leaves, particularly at the base, and star-shaped, red, pink and white flowers. Modern dwarf strains have less scent. Grow in sun or light shade in rich compost and feed regularly throughout the summer. Treat as a half-hardy annual: raise from seed in early spring and plant out after the frosts.

Pelargonium (25)
Pelargonium/geranium

The best pelargoniums for window boxes, pots and hanging baskets are the ivy-leaved, Swiss Balcony and zonal types. These have white to bright red flowers with pink and mauve intermediates. Repot in late autumn and cut down by half before overwintering in a frost-free place. Cut back to a healthy eye in late spring before taking out after all risk of frost has passed. Pelargoniums do best if their roots are restricted and kept on the dry side. Too rich a compost and excess water make for overlush leaves and few flowers.

Petunia × *hybrida* (23)

A jolly group of brightly-coloured half-hardy annuals. *Grandiflora* and *multiflora* strains have, respectively, large and smaller trumpet-shaped flowers. Colours vary from pure white through red, pink, purple and yellow. Some are striped, some frilly, some double. Plant 9 inches (23cm) apart in light sandy compost.

Primula (18)
Primroses and polyanthus

Modern primula strains flower early, have a long season and are available in many colours – perfect for the pot and window box garden. Sow in spring and prick out in peat-based compost, kept cool and shaded until big enough to be planted out. Give high potash feed when the roots are well formed. Sprinkle gravel around the neck of the container to prevent rot.

Tropaeolum majus (22)
Nasturtium

Trailing half-hardy annuals growing to 6–10 feet (1.8–3m) with yellow, red or orange flowers and an exotic spur. The leaves are flat, round plates, bright green except in the cultivar 'Alaska', which has white marbling. Flowers and leaves make a peppery addition to a summer salad. After last frosts, sow in situ in sun. Too much water and fertilizer results in many leaves and few flowers.

Vinca minor (19)
Lesser periwinkle

An evergreen trailing perennial with small, oval, shiny, dark leaves and bright bluey-mauve, star-shaped flowers in early to mid-spring. Tolerates shade, so is useful in a dark town garden. Also suitable for steep banks. Grow in well-drained soil. Cultivars range in colour from white 'Alba' to plum-purple (double) 'Multiplex'. Some have variegated leaves.

Viola × *wittrockiana* (13)
Pansies

The flat-faced flowers of pansies start flowering in mid or late winter and help to cheer the cold months. Colours include white, yellow, rusty-red, mauvey-blue, purple-black; some are bicoloured. They need a well-drained but not dry soil that contains some humus. Sow winter-flowering strains in late summer and plant out in flowering positions in autumn. Deadhead to extend the flowering season.

VIGOROUS PLANTS FOR PERGOLAS

1 *Clematis macropetala*
2 *Hedera helix* (ivy)
3 *Laburnum × watereri* 'Vossii'
4 *Clematis montana rubens*
5 *Lonicera japonica* 'Halliana' (honeysuckle)

6 *Hedera helix* 'Tricolor' (ivy)
7 *Wisteria sinensis*
8 *Clematis × jackmanii*
9 *Rosa* 'Golden Showers'
10 *Polygonum aubertii*

SPRING

11 *Humulus lupulus* 'Aureus' (golden hop)
12 *Rosa* 'Dorothy Perkins'
13 *Rosa* 'Danse du Feu'
14 *Rosa* 'Félicité Perpétue'
15 *Rosa* 'Lawrence Johnston'

16 *Passiflora caerulea* (passion flower)
17 *Clematis tangutica*
18 *Akebia quinata*
19 *Tilia × euchlora* (lime)
20 *Vitis coignetiae*

S U M M E R A U T U M N W I N T E R

VIGOROUS PLANTS FOR PERGOLAS

This sections consists of vigorous plants suitable for pergolas, arbours and arcades. They require plenty of light and water to grow well. Some are better suited to the shady side of the structure, and some need careful pruning to prevent them from running riot and blocking out light and air. If you select carefully, you can grow several of these plants together for year-round interest.

Akebia quinata (18)

A strong-growing, twining shrub, which grows up to 33 feet (10m). It is hardy and evergreen in mild climates, deciduous in cold. Fragrant racemes of dark red to purple flowers grow on the previous season's wood from mid-spring on. After a mild spring and long hot summer it will produce dark purple, sausage-shaped fruits, which split to reveal black seeds and white pulpy flesh. It has been suggested that two plants from distinct origins should be grown together to improve fruiting, as clonal flowers may be self-sterile. Grows in most soils, in sun or shade. Prune after flowering but leave some flowering branches if fruiting is likely.

Clematis × jackmanii (8)

A mid-19th century hybrid, origin of the popular group of large-flowered clematis. Masses of deep purple blooms, 4–5 inches (10–13cm) across, appear on current season's growth early to mid-summer; flowering continues to autumn if the weather is favourable. Will grow in most positions, given plenty of moisture. The cultivar 'Superba' is similar to the original cross, with slightly deeper and larger flowers. 'Victoria' is a paler purple, 'Perle d'Azur' is pale blue, 'Comtesse de Bouchaud' pink and 'Gipsy Queen' violet-purple. All should be pruned back to 3 feet (1m) from the ground in late winter or early spring.

Clematis macropetala (1)

An early-flowering native of Siberia and Kansu province (China). Grows to 10 feet (3m), with delicate leaves, of three leaflets, each subdivided into three. Small, double, violet-blue, nodding flowers grow in the axils on previous season's growth from mid- to late-spring, with a few subsequent flowers on the current season's vines. Gives a good show of seed heads in autumn, if some flowering stems are left to mature, but most should be cut down to promote growth for the following season's blooms. Popular cultivars are the clear blue 'Maidwell Hall', and 'Markham's Pink'.

Clematis montana rubens (4)

A natural pink form of *Clematis montana*, the most vigorous of all clematis. Control by pruning as soon as the short flowering season is over (mid to late spring), to prevent rampant growth, which can block gutters, lift roof tiles and smother other plants. All cultivars of *C. montana* are scented, some particularly so. Pink forms tend to be paler if grown in shade.

Clematis tangutica (17)

A late-flowering, yellow species which reaches 15 feet (4.5m), often confused with the closely related, but less common, *C. orientalis* and *C. tibetana vernayi*. All have yellow to greenish-yellow, nodding flowers from mid-summer on, followed by silky seed heads. Named forms will be true to type only if purchased from a reputable nursery that propagates from cuttings, not from seed. They include: 'Gravetye Variety', 'Bill Mackenzie' and 'Orange Peel'. Prune in late winter before growth starts, but not too hard as this tends to suppress flowering.

Hedera helix (2)
Ivy

Although best suited to growing on walls, this well-known plant can be a great asset on a pergola as a background to other plants and for winter foliage. A woodland species, it does best on the shady side of the supporting structure and prefers alkaline soil. It is long-lived and can reach great heights. In the juvenile stage the leaves are typically lobe-shaped; in the adult stage the leaves are more rounded and the plant bears flowers (a great source of pollen for bees when there is little else around), followed by clusters of black fruit. Prune in early spring to contain and shape the plant.

Hedera helix 'Tricolor' (6)

One of the many attractively variegated forms of ivy, with broad, creamy-white margins, often tinged pink in winter. Other cultivars include the yellow centred 'Goldheart', the dark green 'Atropurpurea' (turning deep purple in winter), the light green to yellow bird's foot ivy 'Pedata', the similarly shaped variegated form 'Caenwoodiana Aurea' and the narrowly lobed 'Digitata'. Cut out any branches that revert to species, as they tend to be more vigorous and will outgrow the chosen cultivar.

Humulus lupulus 'Aureus' (11)
Golden hop

The golden form of the European native herbaceous perennial climber grows to at least 20 feet (6m) within the growing season, making a mat of twining stems with five- to seven-lobed palmate leaves. The small autumnal flowers have no petals: the showy part consists of wide bracts clustered together to form cone-like spikes. These are used to flavour beer and dry well when picked to make attractive winter indoor decorations. Hops grow best in a reasonably sunny position provided that the soil is fairly fertile and moist. Propagate by division in spring. The Japanese hop (*Humulus japonicus*) has an attractive form, 'Variegatus', which is splashed white.

Laburnum × watereri (3)

One of the best and most commonly grown forms of this hybrid laburnum is the cultivar 'Vossii'. It has 2 feet (60cm) long racemes of deep yellow pea-flowers in early summer and pretty leaves with three separate leaflets. Though not a climber, it can be trained to make an attractive arch or pergola-like tunnel. Remove the seed pods soon after blooming, as they tend to reduce the vigour of the tree and are poisonous. The tree grows in any reasonably well drained soil.

Lonicera japonica 'Halliana' (5)
Honeysuckle

In perfect conditions this honeysuckle is rampant, and even in slightly adverse conditions will grow strongly enough to cover a pergola or hide unsightly structures. It has bright green leaves and white, strongly fragrant flowers, which age to an orangey-yellow, throughout the summer, followed by small, shiny black berries. It will grow in most reasonable soils but is not perfectly hardy in the coldest areas. Prune stems back hard in early spring to keep the plant within bounds and prevent it from developing a knotted mass high up.

Passiflora caerulea (16)
Passion flower

A native of South America but surprisingly hardy, particularly if grown in well-drained soil with some protection at its base. Even if checked by cold weather, it usually grows back from the base making 10–15 feet (3–5m) of growth in a good season. Evergreen in very mild districts, the leaves have five to seven finger-like, dark green lobes. The fascinating flowers have a tiered structure. Spanish missionaries likened the flower parts to the instruments of Christ's Passion: hence the common name. The corona (crown of thorns) is striped purple, white and blue, against greenish-white tepals (the apostles); the stigmas (the three nails) are creamy white. The flowers stay closed on dull days. The fruit, in good years, is orange and egg-shaped; it is not always edible. 'Constance Elliott' is a beautiful all-white cultivar.

Polygonum aubertii (10)

P. aubertii is distinguished from the commoner true Russian vine, P. baldschuanicum, by the minute hairs on the stems, which can be felt but barely seen. Both grow remarkably quickly, covering most structures in just a few seasons, and reaching about 25 feet (12m). The flowers are creamy-white, in panicles, which give the plant a frothy look throughout the summer. The leaves are the typical heart shape of the genus. Both grow in any soil but poor, dry soils need enriching with a reasonably moist loam for full vigour. Prune at the beginning of the growing season, cutting some vines down to the ground to avoid the plant becoming a tangled mass high up.

Rosa 'Danse du Feu' (13)

Also known as 'Spectacular', this modern climber suits both its names. Masses of bright scarlet, slightly scented, semi-double flowers appear in early summer, with a few recurrent blooms through the rest of the summer. The foliage is, at first, bronzey, turning bright glossy green in striking contrast with the flowers. A strong climber, it will reach 10 feet (3m) in well-drained, humus-rich, well-balanced soil. Suitable for growing up pillars, it does well in a slightly shady position. Prune unsightly dead flowers and remove dead or diseased wood in late winter.

Rosa 'Dorothy Perkins' (12)

An old rose, introduced by the American nurserymen, Jackson & Perkins, in 1901. Vigorous, reaching 12 feet (4m), with clusters of small, double, clear pink flowers which are neither scented nor repeat-flowering but have great charm. This cultivar is particularly suited to pergolas or open structures, as it is prone to mildew if not grown in a sunny, airy position. Minimize the risk of mildew by spraying with a proprietary fungicide in spring. Remove all dead heads in summer and prune dead and diseased branches in spring.

Rosa 'Félicité Perpétue' (14)

Introduced in 1827 by Monsieur Jacques, the gardener of the Duc d'Orléans. One of its parents was the European Rosa sempervirens, hence it is nearly evergreen. It makes long shoots up to 18 feet (5.5m) in length, so is ideal for a pergola or for growing up an old tree. The leaves are small, dark and shiny green. The flowers are pleasantly fragrant, small, creamy-white with a hint of pink, and grow in large clusters; they have a short season, later than most, from mid to late summer. It is easy to grow, tolerating even light shade. Flowering is most prolific if the prickly, overlapping growths are left unpruned, cutting out only the very old and diseased wood.

Rosa 'Golden Showers' (9)

A rather stiff, upright modern climber, best for growing up pergola pillars, reaching 6–10 feet (2–3m). One of the most popular yellow roses, as it flowers almost continuously from early to late summer and will grow in most conditions, tolerating wind, rain and some shade. The leaves are light green and the large flowers a rich lemon colour fading, particularly in strong sunlight, to cream, with a faint lemony scent. Deadhead throughout the summer and cut out dead or diseased branches in winter. Cut one stem back to ground occasionally to promote new growth.

Rosa 'Lawrence Johnston' (15)

Major Johnston rescued this spectacular cultivar from a French hybridist who was not interested in it, and the original is still growing in the garden at Hidcote in Gloucestershire. It is very vigorous, reaching some 20 feet (6m), with a wealth of flowers in early summer. Sparse flowering continues until the early autumn. The loosely double blooms, strongly scented, are a bright, unfading yellow that contrasts nicely with the clear shiny green leaves. The plant requires little or no pruning. Needs plenty of space.

Tilia × euchlora (19)
Lime

Neither a climber nor a wall shrub, but included here for its use in pleaching and for making into tunnels and arbours. A tall tree, exceeding 50 feet (15m), unless controlled, with somewhat pendulous, lax growth that is easy to train into shape. The leaves are heart-shaped with serrated edges, a warm, rich green above, pale green below so as to make a lively pattern in the wind. The flowers are pale green and fragrant. The fruit is used for making tilleul (lime tea – Proust's favourite infusion). Unlike many limes, this cultivar is not subject to aphids, which drop honeydew to the detriment of underlying plants.

Vitis coignetiae (20)
Crimson glory vine

A spectacular vine, at its most glorious in autumn when the huge leaves turn diverse hues of orange, red and bronze. In spring the leaves are a dull green with a rich, rusty felt of hairs on the underside. They are broadly heart-shaped with three indistinct lobes about 8 inches (20cm) long by 4 inches (10cm) wide but sometimes reaching 12 by 10 inches (30 × 25cm). The vine will grow to an equally phenomenal height – up to 75 feet (22m), given the support of a tree. Over a pergola, prune in early spring; cut back to just above a plump bud.

Wisteria sinensis (7)

Early summer would not be the same without the beautiful purple or white racemes of the wisteria. An iron arbour or pergola will quickly be covered by this vigorous twining climber. It is not particular as to soil, although a good loam is preferable; but it does need full sun to mature and flower successfully and, in colder climates, protection from early frosts. In a tree it will reach 60 to 100 feet (18–30m). To restrict growth, prune annually in late winter, cutting stems back to just above a healthy bud; the leafy shoots should also be reduced in late summer. The heavily scented mauve or lilac flowers are carried in racemes and open before the leaves. The white form is called 'Alba'.

PLANTS FOR HEDGES

1 *Berberis × stenophylla*
2 *Elaeagnus pungens* 'Maculata'
3 *Camellia × williamsii*
4 *Taxus baccata* (yew)
5 *Carpinus betulus* (hornbeam)

6 *Osmanthus delavayi*
7 *Thuja plicata* (Western red cedar)
8 *Prunus lusitanica* (Portuguese laurel)
9 *Rosa pimpinellifolia* (burnet)

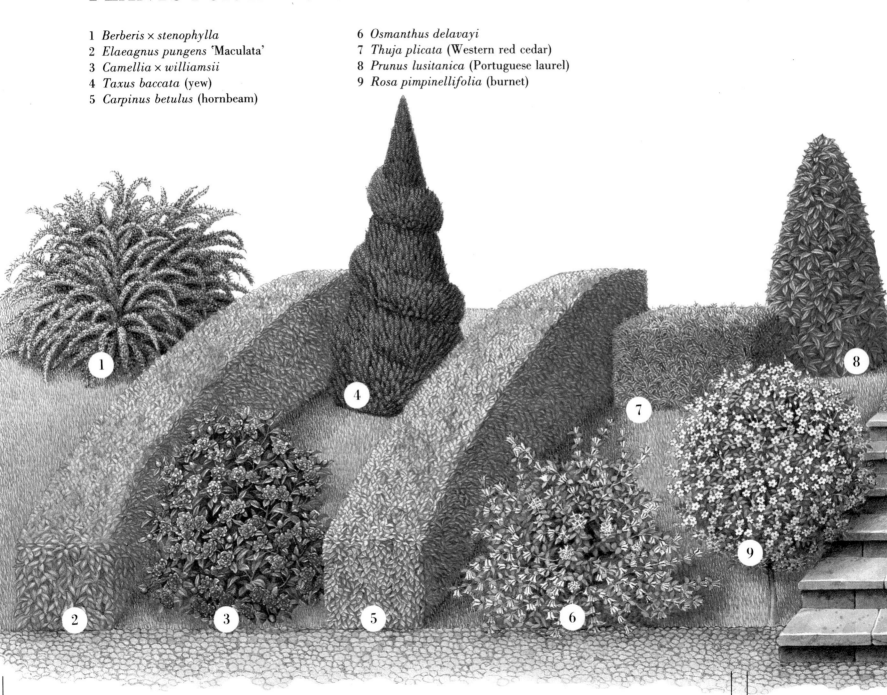

SPRING

10 *Viburnum opulus* (guelder rose)
11 *Ligustrum ovalifolium* 'Aureum'
(golden privet)
12 *Cupressus macrocarpa* (Monterey cypress)
13 *Hypericum* 'Hidcote'

14 *Fagus sylvatica* (beech)
15 *Buxus sempervirens* (box)
16 *Rosa rugosa*
17 *Ilex × altaclerensis* (holly)
18 *Viburnum tinus*

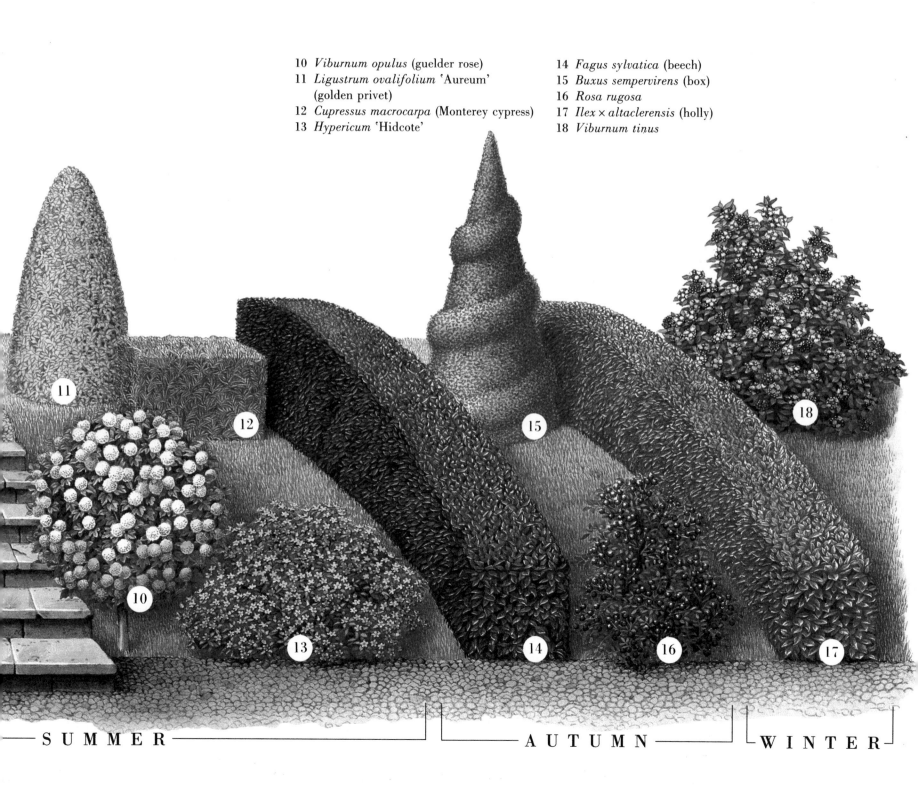

SUMMER — AUTUMN — WINTER

PLANTS FOR HEDGES

The shrubby plants described in this section are suitable for making either formal or informal hedges. Your choice will depend on many factors, including the purpose the hedge has to serve, growing conditions, space available and speed of growth required. Some hedging plants have fruits or flowers that provide special interest at certain times of year.

EVERGREEN

Buxus sempervirens (15)
Box

A small, round-leaved evergreen shrub which stands severe pruning and is ideal for topiary and hedge-making. It prefers warm, dry soils, but is very adaptable, coping with most soils and positions (sun or shade) and withstanding atmospheric pollution and salt. Prune any time during summer to keep it neat and trim. Grows slowly, so large hedges are rarely seen, although it will reach 8 feet (2.5m) or more in time. The variety *B. sempervirens suffruticosa*, with smaller leaves, is good for edging.

Cupressus macrocarpa (12)
Monterey cypress

A fast-growing conifer, useful where a quick screen is needed. Will grow by the sea or in towns, and tolerates dry, sandy or chalky soils. It needs space and should be trimmed in spring or midsummer, but not too severely as the young growth is prone to frost damage. The smaller cultivars of *Chamaecyparis lawsoniana* or the much-used × *Cupressocyparis leylandii* are hardier.

Elaeagnus pungens 'Maculata' (2)

A robust shrub that makes a good screen, suitable for towns and seaside gardens and tolerant of shade. The leaves of the species are dark grey-green above, silvery grey beneath; the leaves of the cultivar have a central golden yellow splash. The young shoots are covered with fine, rusty-brown hairs. In late autumn, highly fragrant, white flowers cover the bush, subsisting for a month or two. Prune lightly in late summer to shape the plant and remove weak stems but take care not to cut out too many flowering branches.

Ilex × *altaclerensis* (17)
Holly

Hollies make excellent dense hedges. *Ilex* × *altaclerensis* reaches 18 feet (5.5m), with variegated, more or less spiny leaves and plenty of berries: among the best cultivars are 'Golden King' and 'Camelliifolia'. *Ilex aquifolium* and its cultivars are rather more prickly to prune. Both thrive in well-drained, light soils but tolerate most soil types, shade and sun, salt and atmospheric pollution. The North American species require acid soils and a dry continental climate (cold, dry winters, hot summers); they include the deciduous *I. verticillata*, particularly the cultivar 'Christmas Cheer'; and the blue hollies, *I.* × *meserveae*, 'Blue Princess' and 'Blue Stallion'.

Ligustrum ovalifolium 'Aureum' (11)
Golden privet

The semi-evergreen privet makes a fast growing hedge that is not fussy as to soil or location. Its chief drawback is the need for frequent clipping throughout the growing season. The golden form has attractive deep yellow, sometimes green-centred, leaves. It makes a good standard: a tall central stem can be quickly obtained and the head responds well to frequent pruning. With regular feeding and watering, it can be grown in a pot.

Prunus lusitanica (8)
Portuguese laurel

This handsome evergreen has shiny, dark green, oval, pointed leaves on red stems. It is happy on most soils, even shallow and alkaline. Planted at 3 feet (1m) intervals it makes a good hedge up to 15 feet (4.5m) tall and stands hard pruning which should be done in early spring, using secateurs. It will bear racemes of white flowers in early summer if trimming is less severe. Can be grown as a standard. The cherry laurel, *P. laurocerasus*, has larger, light green leaves but is less hardy, and unhappy on shallow soils. With both laurels, take care not to let the top overshadow the base or the base will become bare.

Taxus baccata (4)
Yew

The perfect foil and background for shrubs, herbaceous perennials, sculptures and ornaments, this remarkable evergreen is equally happy in acid and alkaline soils, sun or shade. With an annual top dressing of fertilizer, it will grow quite rapidly, making a substantial hedge. Both the leaves and seeds (protected by a fleshy red aril) are deadly poisonous. The species has black-green foliage but there are several attractive golden forms. The hybrid cultivar *T.* × *media* 'Hicksii' is more consistently hardy, and able to withstand low temperatures. Both are suitable for topiary. Trim in late summer.

Thuja plicata (7)
Western red cedar

This hardy evergreen conifer is one of the best hedging plants available, provided that it is protected from drought and frost during the establishment period. It has a good bright green colour all year, grows fast and responds well to regular clipping – a task rewarded by the orange-peel scent of the leaves when bruised. A more hardy species is the American Arborvitae *T. occidentalis*, which tolerates colder, wetter soils but grows more slowly and has duller leaves. Both should be trimmed in late summer.

DECIDUOUS

Carpinus betulus (5)
Hornbeam

A small to medium tree that has long been used for hedges, quite hardy, able to grow on most soils including chalk and clay and tolerant of atmospheric pollution. Its delicate pale green, heavily veined leaves unfurl in the spring and turn brown in the autumn, staying on the tree throughout winter if clipped late in the season.

Fagus sylvatica (14)
Beech

Similar in appearance to hornbeam, beech differs in not liking damp soil and prefering well-drained light (sandy or chalky) soils. It is more susceptible to late spring frosts and has larger, smoother leaves which, like those of the hornbeam, remain on the hedge throughout the winter, provided that it has been trimmed in late summer or early autumn. Copper beech makes an attractive alternative. Raised from seed, beeches tend to vary greatly in habit, colour and time of emergence, but this only adds to their charm.

FLOWERING (DECIDUOUS AND EVERGREEN)

Berberis × *stenophylla* (1)

This evergreen hybrid makes a beautiful shower of golden-orange flowers in spring, followed in summer by blue fruit. It has graceful, arching stems with narrow, holly-like leaves about 1 inch (2.5cm) long. Cut back branches to stimulate new growth for next year's crop of flowers, but leave some to bear fruit. Some stems will need cutting right down to prevent the plant from becoming a tangled mass.

Camellia × *williamsii* (3)

One of the best and hardiest of the camellias, though not suitable for extremely cold and exposed positions. An evergreen with dark glossy green leaves above, pale matt green below. Will reach 8 feet (2.5m) or more in mild areas. The free-flowering blooms fall off the shrub rather than turning brown on the plant; they vary in colour from white as in the cultivar 'Francis Hanger', pale pink as in 'J.C. Williams' and darker pink as in the best of all, 'Donation'.

Hypericum 'Hidcote' (13)

An excellent low-growing, semi-evergreen shrub that has slender, arching, brown stems to about 5 feet (1.5m). The leaves are bright apple-green and throughout summer the large flowers are a beautiful yellow with a prominent bunch of golden stamens. It is not demanding, growing equally well on humus-rich and dry soils. Cut hard back in late winter or early spring to maintain an even shape.

Osmanthus delavayi (6)

This Chinese species is a slow grower, particularly in cold areas, reaching about 6 feet (2m). However, it is a delight in spring when covered in small white flowers that fill the air with their enticing fragrance. It is evergreen with tiny, dark green, oval leaves that have serrated edges. Requires a minimum of pruning in mid-summer. *O. heterophyllus* is slightly more hardy, has holly-like leaves and flowers in autumn; the blooms are equally fragrant.

Rosa pimpinellifolia (9)
Burnet or Scotch rose

This hardy species grows 3–4 feet (1–1.2m) high and will thrive on dry, well-drained soils. It occurs wild in sand or shingle near the sea or inland on limestone. The suckering, upright, spiny stems, sometimes invasive, carry tightly set leaves made of tiny, deep green leaflets. The pale yellow, creamy white or pale pink flowers are borne in late spring or early summer. Dead and damaged stems should be cut out during the winter.

Rosa rugosa (16)

One of the most rugged of the roses. Makes a dense attractive hedge, particularly in early summer when in flower and in the autumn when covered in hips. The solid, thorny stems reach about 5 feet (1.5m) and are covered with downy, well-veined leaves that frequently turn yellow in the autumn. The deep pink flowers are 3 inches (8cm) or more across, with cream stamens, and very fragrant. The hips are bright red, 1 inch (2.5cm) round, flattened at the top. Two of the best cultivars are the famous 'Roseraie de l'Haÿ' which has rich crimson purple flowers and the clear pink 'Fru Dagmar Hastrupp'. The white 'Blanc Double de Coubert' is taller and less compact and therefore not so well suited for use as a hedge. Prune dead and damaged stems in the winter.

Viburnum opulus (10)
Guelder rose

This vigorous shrub makes an attractive screen at most times of year. The leaves are three- to five-lobed, pale green until the autumn when they take on rich tints. In early summer the shrub is covered with flat corymbs of fertile flowers amid white ray florets. These are followed by bunches of bright, translucent red berries. The cultivar 'Sterile' has no fertile flowers (and therefore no berries); instead, the inflorescences form great balls of infertile, white florets, hence the common name "snowball". 'Compactum' is a neater, less vigorous form which doesn't require the pruning necessary to contain the species. 'Aureum' has golden leaves throughout the year. 'Fructu-luteo' and 'Xanthocarpum' each have yellow fruit.

Viburnum tinus (18)
Laurustinus

This accomodating evergreen shrub has all the qualities: it is resistant to atmospheric pollution, salt spray and shade; it has dark green, glossy foliage and bears flattened cymes of white flowers (pink in bud) from late autumn to mid spring; the blue fruits, ripening to black, often overlap with the flowers. As with any informal hedging plant, minimal pruning is required to keep it in shape and remove weak growth. The cultivar 'Eve Price' was selected for its dense compact habit; it has smaller leaves and pale pink flowers (deeper in bud).

TERRACES AND STEPS

TERRACES

Terraces will give form and substance to a sloping garden. Variations in width and height will add to the interest.

First, you must measure the slope that you wish to terrace. There are several ways to do this. One way is by using water in a hosepipe, as illustrated (right). The height of the drop is the height of the water level above the ground at the foot of the slope, minus the height of the water from the ground at the top of the slope.

Another method is to use a series of boning rods (stakes with short pieces of wood nailed across near the top and bottom at right angles) with a straight-edged plank and a spirit level. Fix a short boning rod in the ground at the top of the slope and a longer one further down. Lay the plank between the two rods at the top and adjust the depth of one of the rods until the spirit level shows you that the plank is level. Then place a third rod lower down the slope, lining its top cross-piece by eye with the

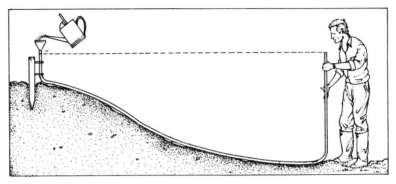

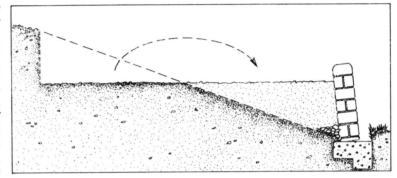

bottom cross-piece of the second rod. Proceed in this way all down the slope. Then measure the various vertical dimensions and add them all up. Don't forget to subtract the height of the cross-piece from the ground at the top of the slope.

Once you have decided how many terraces you want, and what height and width they are to be, you will be ready to start the hard work. First, remove the top soil over the whole site to a depth of about 8 inches (20cm) and store it in a convenient place. Then mark out where the retaining wall for each terrace is to be. First, construct the wall nearest the house (see page 64). A week later, level the soil on the cut and fill principle (left). Remember that you will need steps to get from one level to the next. When each terrace is level you can replace the top soil.

Even moving a small volume of earth may be laborious: do not tackle the job unless you are sure you can cope with it. It might be worth paying a contractor to move the earth mechanically.

STEPS

Steps can be of concrete, bricks, paving stones, railway sleepers or logs. They can be formal or informal, broad and shallow or narrow and deep. But whatever the style you choose, the steps will need to be comfortable to walk on and well constructed.

The first thing to decide is how high the steps are going to be. It is inadvisable to make them higher than 7 inches (18cm) or shallower than 4 inches (10cm). The proportions of riser (height) to tread (depth from front to back) should follow this formula: depth = 26 inches (66cm) − (2 × height). After measuring the total height of the slope (as described above), you can work out how many steps you need. For example, a fall of 5 feet (1.5m)

will require 12 steps of 5 inches (60 inches ÷ 5); following the formula given above, the treads will need to be about 16 inches (40cm) deep; hence, the length of the flight needs to be 16 feet (4.8m). If this does not suit the site, you must adjust the measurements accordingly.

Once the measurements have been worked out, you can cut out the steps and build them up. Starting at the

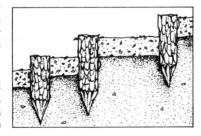

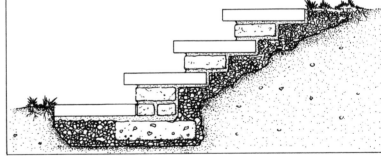

bottom of the steps, dig a trench at least 4 inches (10cm) deep and as wide as the steps and fill it with a concrete base. Allow to set for a whole day before you build the first riser on and against a bed of mortar; then lay the first tread on a bed of mortar; and so on (diagram, above). The treads must slope slightly

forward so that water runs off.

An attractive flight of informal steps can be made using a row of wooden logs to form the risers, as shown in the diagram, left. In a woodland garden you could use gravel, or perhaps earth and bark flakes, built up behind the logs to form the treads.

STRUCTURES AND SUPPORTS

PERGOLAS

Pergolas are best kept simple, particularly if their chief purpose is to support plants. They should be at least 6 feet (2 metres) wide. Whatever their design, they must be constructed to last. The wood must be treated in non-toxic preservative.

If the uprights are of wood, they should be sturdy, 3 inches (8cm) or 4 inches (10cm) square, and firmly held in the ground in a concrete collar about 12 inches (30cm) square. Two methods of construction are shown in the diagrams, below right. In the first method, the post is set about 2 feet (60cm) in the ground. Nails driven into the lower part of the post increase the concrete's grip. Another way to improve stability is to use an H-shaped bracket: the post is fastened into the bracket with bolts and then sunk into the concrete. To ensure that a puddle does not form at the base of the post, it is advisable to make a mound of soil or concrete.

The cross-pieces can be of 3 × 2 inch (7.5 × 5cm) wood. The diagram, below left, shows a reliable way to attach them. They should be strong enough to support themselves and the plants intended for them without bowing. As a rule of thumb, they should be able to support the weight of an adult man.

If the pergola abuts a wall, you can slot the cross-pieces on the wall side into metal brackets fixed in place by long screws and wall plugs. A small pergola can be made of peeled larch poles notched and nailed together.

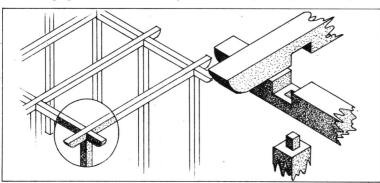

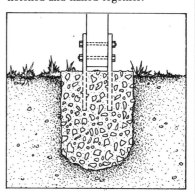

TRELLISES AND WALL SUPPORTS

A trellis can be freestanding (fixed to posts inserted as described above) or wall-mounted. If on a wall, the trellis should be held away from the brickwork on pieces of timber (spacers) to allow for ventilation, prevent rotting of the wood and facilitate pruning. A trellis panel hinged to a wall-mounted length of wood at the bottom and hooked onto the wall at the top can be lowered periodically, with plants still in place, so that you can repaint the wall or attend to the plants.

Various methods for tying climbers to a wall trellis (1, 2), fence (3) or masonry wall (4, 5) are shown in the diagrams, right. The method you choose will depend on the weight of the plant, the type of stem and the method of climbing. Check ties occasionally to ensure that they will not strangle the growing plants.

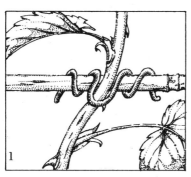

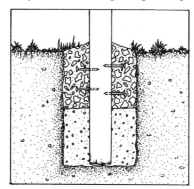

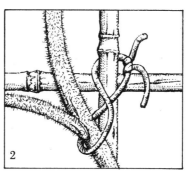

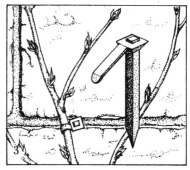

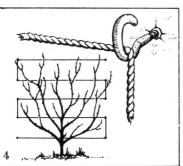

KEY

1 Green plastic-coated wire, sold in garden stores
2 Strong twine or tarred string
3 Wall nail with flexible strip of lead, for woody stems
4 Nylon cord or twine on screw eyes, for light climbers
5 Galvanized wire on vine eyes (not more than 6 feet/1.8m apart)

PRUNING

Pruning in the vertical garden is probably the single most important task – to encourage maximum flowering either in the same or the subsequent year, to remove dead or diseased branches, or to shape and contain plants that in a small garden with a favourable microclimate can become rampant if you are not ruthless.

It is important that you have the right tools for the job. Invest in good-quality implements and look after them.

Secateurs are the standard pruning tool. The anvil type (1 in the diagram, right) has one sharp cutting edge that cuts against a flattened blade; it has straight metal handles. The parrot-billed type (3) has two cutting blades that cross each other like scissors; the shaped handles are coated in plastic for comfort. Secateurs are not suitable for cutting large stems, and will be damaged if you try. Always buy the biggest and best you can afford. They will need regular oiling to prevent them from rusting, and the blades will need sharpening and sometimes replacing.

Knives can also be useful tools for light pruning, as it is always better to

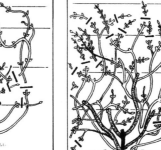

have a clean cut than a jagged tear.

For thicker branches and stems it is useful to have long-handled lopping shears (8) which have a good leverage and can easily cut branches up to $1\frac{3}{4}$ inches (4cm) thick. For the thickest branches a pruning saw will be necessary (4).

For the tallest plants, long-handled pruners will be useful (5). They can extend up to 10 feet (3m) long and will cut stems up to $1\frac{1}{2}$ inches (3cm) thick.

KEY
1 Secateurs (anvil type)
2 Secateurs (curved blade)
3 Secateurs (scissor type)
4 Pruning saw
5 Long-handled pruner (in three sections)
6 Pruning knife
7 Pruning knife
8 Long-handled lopping shears
9 Hand shears

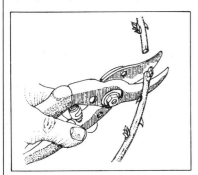

Always prune $\frac{1}{4}$ inch (5mm) above and gently sloping away from the selected bud. If the cut is too low, the bud may be damaged. If the cut is too high, the stem may die back. The more of the shoot that is removed, the stronger the growth will be.

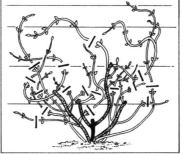

Climbers and wall shrubs that bear flowers on the current year's growth should be pruned hard back in late winter/early spring. Some can be cut down to near ground level. Others should be allowed to develop a strong framework before cutting back.

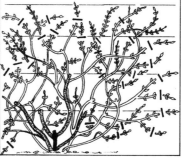

Climbers and wall shrubs that flower on the previous year's shoots should be pruned soon after flowering in late spring/early summer to allow young shoots to grow up and flower the following year. These include jasmine, forsythia, ornamental quince.

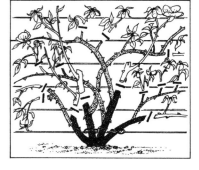

Climbers and wall shrubs that need only deadheading to prevent seed production and strengthen growth, and to keep the plant in shape. These include Hydrangea petiolaris and most roses. Diseased or dead stems should be removed promptly.

GLOSSARY

Terms in CAPITAL LETTERS cross-refer to other glossary entries.

Annual A plant whose lifespan – from seed to flowering and death – is less than one year.

Anthers The pollen-bearing part of the stamen, usually with two lobes each containing two pollen sacks.

Arbour A small-scale garden shelter usually consisting of a timber or trellised frame with plants climbing all over it.

Axil buds The buds that are found in the angle formed by the junction of leaf and stem.

Bedding plants Plants that are planted and displayed for one season only – as opposed to border plants, which are permanent. They may be ANNUALS, BIENNIALS or TENDER PERENNIALS.

Biennial A plant that requires two growing seasons to complete its life cycle; for example, a foxglove. Leaves are formed during the first year and flowers and seeds the following year.

Bulb A modified shoot consisting of a basal fleshy stem or plate that develops roots below and has closely folded-over leaves above: these contain reserve food and protect the flower bud.

Calyx The outer layer of floral leaves. They are normally green but occasionally, as in clematis, coloured.

Clairvoyée A window in a wall or gate through which can be glimpsed the view beyond, either in or out of the garden. The opening may be fitted with a grill.

Clone One of a group of identical plants all raised from a single parent plant by vegetative propagation.

Compost A rooting medium for plants, providing suitable drainage, aeration, and nutrients for maximum growth. Normally used in containers.

Conifer Any cone-bearing tree; also includes yews and junipers, which have fleshy fruits. Most conifers are evergreen, with scaly, needle-like or strap-shaped leaves.

Cultivar An identified strain or HYBRID that has arisen either naturally in the garden or in the wild, or by purposeful breeding and selection.

Deadheading Removing faded flowers from a plant, partly for its appearance but also to prevent it from spending its energy on producing seeds. Deadheading often produces a better crop of flowers the following year; and in some cases encourages more flowers to appear in the same year.

Deciduous A plant that loses all its leaves at one time of the year, usually late autumn.

Division A method of propagation in which the crown of the plant is split into several sections, each with roots, and replanted. Normally, a method for HERBACEOUS PERENNIALS.

Dwarfing rootstock A ROOTSTOCK of diminished vigour, which reduces the growth of the selected scion.

Espalier A lattice-work of wood or wires on which to train trees. Also, a method of training fruit trees, by selecting lateral branches to grow horizontally on each side of the main stem.

Evergreen A plant that keeps its foliage for at least a year. A wintergreen retains its leaves for one year only.

Fastigiate A variety of tree or shrub with erect branches: for example, Irish yew.

Gazebo A garden pavilion; strictly, one designed to offer a view.

Half-hardy Describes those plants that will survive the winter if given some kind of protection, either against a wall or under polythene or glass.

Hardy Describes a plant capable of surviving for the whole of its lifespan without any protection from frost. In hot climates, hardiness may refer to a plant's resistance to drought.

Herbaceous A PERENNIAL plant that dies back to the ground level each autumn or winter. The term also applies to borders that are filled largely or entirely with such plants.

Herbicide A chemical substance that kills weeds. Some act on contact (eg paraquat), other are taken in through the plant (eg simazine).

Hybrid A natural or man-made cross between two species or genera.

Inflorescence The part of the plant that bears the flowers.

Microclimate A climate particular to a specific situation (eg against a wall or hedge) which differs from the overall climate of the area.

Perennial A plant that lives for more than two years. Often applied exclusively to HERBACEOUS perennials.

Pergola A walk of pillars and cross members with plants trained to grow up over it.

Pinnate Describes a leaf that is composed of opposite leaflets along a central stalk.

Pleaching Training the branches of trees along wires to make a narrow hedge, usually above bare trunks. Species most commonly pleached include lime, hornbeam and maple.

Pollinator A second strain planted alongside the cultivated species to ensure transfer of pollen from one to another. Used most often in fruit cultivation when successful pollination is essential for a good crop.

Potager The French term for a vegetable garden.

Potash The mineral form of the metal element potassium – one of the substances essential to plant growth.

Propagation The production of a new plant from an existing one, either sexually (by seeds) or vegetatively (eg by cuttings).

Raceme An inflorescence composed of flowers on stalks along a single main stem.

Rambler A plant, especially a rose, that has long, lax stems and is essentially droopy in habit.

Rhizomes Stems that grow horizontally below ground level.

Rootstock Root or plant on which can be grafted certain species that are difficult to PROPAGATE on their own roots.

Self-clinging Describes a climber that does not require support to grow, as it attaches itself by means of short roots (ivy) or sticky, sucker-like pads (virginia creeper).

Self-fertile Describes a plant whose ovules are fertilized by its own pollen and grow into viable seeds.

Self-seeding Describes a plant, usually an annual, that will regenerate from year to year by dispersing its seed around the garden.

Self-sterile Describes a plant whose ovules require pollen from another plant (the pollinator) to grow into viable seeds.

Semi-evergreen Describes a plant that is EVERGREEN in mild areas and DECIDUOUS in colder climes.

Shrub Any plant with many wooded stems, the main ones usually growing from the base.

Slow-release fertilizer A substance that releases the essential nutrients for the growth of a plant over a long period of time – unlike liquid fertilizer, in which the nutrients are available immediately.

Sport The part of a plant that has undergone some spontaneous change (of leaf or flower colour or shape) that is sufficiently desirable to warrant clonal PROPAGATION. The term is also used of the plant thus introduced.

Standard A tree with a clear expanse of bare trunk before the head of branches.

Sub-shrub A small PERENNIAL plant with woody stem bases and soft tips, which die back every year. The term is often used to describe any small SHRUB.

Tender Describes any plants likely to be damaged by low temperatures.

Treillage Trelliswork used to create elaborate screens or architectural structures.

Trompe l'œil A deliberate trick of the eye – for example, the use of false perspective effects to make a garden seem longer.

Tying in The action of securing climbers to a support, either on a wall or any other open structure. It should be done at least once a year.

Versailles caisse A large plant container made of wood, of the type traditionally used in French-style gardens. Often has removable sides to ease repotting and renewal of compost, and sometimes has wheels.

Wall shrub A HALF-HARDY shrub that requires the protection and warmth of a wall to survive the winter in cooler climates.

Zonal A plant part with a region, often ring-like, of a different colour from the remainder. For example, zonal pelargoniums have rings of darker or lighter colour on their leaves.

INDEX

Page numbers in *italics* refer to illustration captions

Acknowledgments

PHOTO CREDITS

Front cover: Michael & Lois Warren
Half-title page: Insight Picture Library/Linda Burgess
Title-page: Tommy Candler
4–5: Philippe Perdereau
Contents: Jerry Harpur (Design: Mirabel Osler)
8: Robert O'Dea
10–11: Philippe Perdereau
12: Jerry Harpur
13: Impact Photos/Pamla Toler
14: Arcaid/Richard Bryant
15L: Kenneth Scowen
15R: Clive Corless
16: Jerry Harpur (Design: Richard Shelbourne)
17: Michael & Lois Warren
18: Insight Picture Library/Michelle Garrett
19L: John Heseltine
19R: Kaleidoscope/Joanne & Jerry Pavia
20: Michael & Lois Warren
21: Michael & Lois Warren
22–23: John Neubauer (Design: Oehme, van Sweden & Associates, Inc.)
23L: Philippe Perdereau
24L: Tommy Candler
24–25: Tommy Candler
26–27: Garden and Landscape Pictures/Margaret Turner
26L: Tania Midgley
27R: Michael & Lois Warren
28–29: Philippe Perdereau
28L: Tania Midgley
28R: Heather Angel
30L: Michael & Lois Warren
30R: Tania Midgley
31: Garden and Landscape Pictures/Margaret Turner
32–33: Jacqui Hurst
32L: Tania Midgley
33: John Neubauer
(Design: Oehme, van Sweden & Associates, Inc.)
34: Garden and Landscape Pictures/Margaret Turner
35: Tania Midgley
36–37: John Neubauer (Design: Oehme, van Sweden & Associates, Inc.)
37: John Neubauer (Design: Wilhelm Wertz)
38L: Philippe Perdereau
38R: Garden and Landscape Pictures/Margaret Turner
39L: Tania Midgley
40–41: Philippe Perdereau
42: S. & O. Mathews
43: Heather Angel
44: Insight Picture Library/Linda Burgess
45: Alan Williams
46: Heather Angel
47: Heather Angel
48–49: Jacqui Hurst
49R: S. & O. Mathews
50: Philippe Perdereau
51L: Clive Corless
51R: Insight Picture Library/Linda Burgess
52: Insight Picture Library/Michelle Garrett
53BL: S. & O. Mathews
53BR: S. & O. Mathews
53T: Tania Midgley
54L: Insight Picture Library/Linda Burgess
54–55: Philippe Perdereau
55R: Tania Midgley
56: S. & O. Mathews
57: Jacqui Hurst
58: Heather Angel
59L: Tania Midgley
59R: S. & O. Mathews
60: S. & O. Mathews
61: Heather Angel
62: Tania Midgley
63: S. & O. Mathews
64: Jacqui Hurst
65: Jacqui Hurst
66–67: Insight Picture Library/Linda Burgess
67B: Insight Picture Library/Linda Burgess
67T: Tania Midgley
68: Elizabeth Whiting & Associates: (Photo: Tim Street-Porter)
69: Insight Picture Library/Michelle Garrett
70–71: John Neubauer (D.C.A. Landscape Associates)
72: Michael & Lois Warren
73: Michael & Lois Warren
74: Garden and Landscape Pictures/Margaret Turner
75: Garden and Landscape Pictures/Margaret Turner
76L: Insight Picture Library/Linda Burgess
76R: Tania Midgley
77: John Heseltine
78: Michael & Lois Warren
78–79: Jerry Harpur (Design: John Patrick)
79: Kaleidoscope/Joanne & Jerry Pavia
80: Michael & Lois Warren
81L: Insight Picture Library/Michelle Garrett
81R: Philippe Perdereau
82–3: Kaleidoscope/Joanne & Jerry Pavia
83: Tania Midgley
84: Tania Midgley
85: Jerry Harpur (Design: John Patrick)
86–87: Philippe Perdereau
87: Impact Photos/Pamla Toler
88–89: Impact Photos/Pamla Toler
90: John Heseltine
91L: S. & O. Mathews
91R: Impact Photos/Pamla Toler
92–93: Insight Picture Library/Linda Burgess
94L: Clive Corless
94R: S. & O. Mathews
95L: Impact Photos/Pamla Toler
95R: Arcaid/Richard Bryant
96L: Elizabeth Whiting and Associates (Photo: Tom Leighton)
96R: Elizabeth Whiting and Associates (Photo: Michael Dunne)
97L: Kaleidoscope/Joanne & Jerry Pavia
97R: Arcaid/Richard Bryant
98–99: Tania Midgley
99: Jacqui Hurst
100: Jerry Harpur (Design: Rev. and Mrs Feast)
100–101: Insight Picture Library/Michelle Garrett
102L: Arcaid/Richard Bryant
102R: Jacqui Hurst
103: John Heseltine
104–105: Tania Midgley
106: Insight Picture Library/Michelle Garrett
107: Jerry Harpur (Design: Paul Bangay, Melbourne)
108: Garden and Landscape Pictures/Margaret Turner (Design: Charles and Maggie Jencks)
109: John Neubauer (D.C.A. Landscape Associates)
110: Robert O'Dea
111L: Garden and Landscape Pictures/Margaret Turner (Design: Edward Hill)
111R: Garden and Landscape Pictures/Margaret Turner (Sir Frederick and Lady Gibberd's Garden)
112L: Insight Picture Library/Michelle Garrett
112R: Robert O'Dea
113L: Heather Angel
113R: Michael & Lois Warren
114–115: Tommy Candler

BIBLIOGRAPHY

Becket, Kenneth A., *Climbing Plants*, Croom Helm, 1983

Evison, Raymond J., *Making the Most of Clematis*, Floraprint, 1983

Grey-Wilson, C., and Matthews, V., *Gardening on Walls*, Collins, 1983

Jekyll, Gertrude, *Wall and Water Garden*, Country Life, 1901

Lloyd, Christopher, *Clematis*, Collins, 1977

Rose, Peter Q., *Climbers and Wall Plants*, Blandford, 1982

Rose, Peter Q., *Ivies*, Blandford, 1980